"**Hard-hitting, gritty, supremely practical.** This book will—simply and directly—help you make more money and move your business to more efficiency. This is not a book on the 'theory of the case.' It's a book on making your small business more profitable—step-by-step, with checklists, examples, and concrete suggestions."

> *- Ralph A. Oliva, Executive Director, Institute for the Study of Business Markets,*
> *Professor of Marketing, Smeal College of Business, Penn State University*

"**When you own your own business,** it's easy to feel overwhelmed by everyday demands. The Customer-Approved Small Business is a great book to keep on your nightstand. If you can find time to read it just five minutes a day, you'll benefit from its practical suggestions and step-by-step exercises. Use it to keep yourself and your business customer-centric!"

> *- Cathy Cooper, Vice President, Marketing, Washington Federal Savings*

"*The Customer-Approved Small Business* **touches on all aspects** of effective customer communication. These areas include vital first impressions, role-playing customer calls, and simple but sometimes forgotten items like clear voice-mail messages and thank-you notes. This is an excellent book for both service and sales professionals. I will recommend it to my management team!"

> *– Richard Jackson, Service Center Executive, ADP Small Business Services*

"**I like this book because its practical insights and strategies** will help any business, large or small, sell more effectively. In business, nothing happens until somebody sells something."

> *– Roy L. Thomasson, Chief Executive Officer, Young Americas Business Trust*

"**Schell's book reveals cutting-edge advice** for best business practices, and will certainly help small-business owners achieve their goals and increase their profits. All they need to do is seize the opportunity to be creative and implement the great ideas in this book."

– Peter Callaghan, Vice President, Sales & Marketing, Maximizer Software Inc.

"**Common sense—but unfortunately, NOT common practice.** This book gives the reader the tools to 'walk the walk.' Schell provides the inside track on how to effectively manage and grow your business—all from the perspective of the people who matter most: the customers."

- Robin Chakrabarti, Regional Vice President & General Manager,
Canadian Springs Water Company, a division of Danone Waters of Canada

"**It would be misleading to use the tired phrase 'a must-read'** for this book. This is a book that belongs on your desk, well-worn, tattered, with Post-It Notes sticking out of selected pages. The checklists, quotes, and suggestions on how to do things better are invaluable. You'll come away with things you can do - today - to make more money, improve efficiency, and reduce the stress in your small business."

– Sai Jiwani Mohamed, COO, Dexior Financial Inc. – A Private Investment Bank

"**I enjoyed this book . . . It's an easy read** and can be used as a step-by-step guide for small business success. Or if you're just looking for nuggets of truth to help take your business to the next level, it has plenty of those, too."

- Lee Lemke, Business Banking Group Manager, Huntington National Bank

THE CUSTOMER-APPROVED SMALL BUSINESS

THE CUSTOMER-

SMALL
BUSINESS

Success Secrets for
Developing Your Business

MICHAEL SCHELL

Approved Publications Inc.

THE CUSTOMER-APPROVED SMALL BUSINESS:
SUCCESS SECRETS FOR DEVELOPING YOUR BUSINESS

Senior Editor: Andy Fielding

Associate Editors: Mitch Merker, Eva Nerelius, Åsa Nerelius, Mark Bourgeois

Published by **Approved Publications Inc.**
Suite 208 - 700 West Pender Street
Vancouver, British Columbia V6C 1G8

Call us toll-free: **1-877-870-0009**
Visit our website: **www.approvedseries.com**

This publication is designed to provide accurate and authoritative information regarding the subject matter it covers. It is sold with the understanding that the publisher is not rendering legal, accounting, or other professional services. If you require legal advice or other assistance, please seek the services of a competent professional. (From A Declaration of Principles jointly adopted by a Committee of the American Bar Association and a Committee of Publishers)

National Library of Canada Cataloguing in Publication Data

Schell, Michael, 1959-

The customer-approved small business: success secrets for developing your business / Michael Schell.

Includes index.

ISBN 0-9731675-3-X

1. Small business. 2. Success in business. I. Title.

HD62.7.S34 2004   658.02'2   C2004-904392-7

Cover design: Rocks-DeHart Public Relations

Interior design: Andy Fielding

PRINTED IN CANADA

For my amazing mother, Angela Hannaford, for instilling in me her vibrant love of life and her belief in unlimited possibility.

You must have your heart in your business and your business in your heart.

— Thomas J. Watson, Sr.

I skate where the puck is going to be, not where it has been.

— Wayne Gretzky

Contents

PART 3 Tying It All Together   99

Gratitude

g

I've been extremely fortunate to have the help of some exceptional people without whom the Approved™ Series would not have been possible.

Jason Foyle, a valued friend, fellow musician, and fellow director of Approved Group Inc., is the original investor in the Approved Series vision and continues to motivate our team and support our collective goals.

Mitch Merker, my valued friend and business partner, editor, and vice president of The Approved Group Inc. His dedication to our mutual vision has been rock-solid.

Eva Nerelius, a valued friend and the business operations manager of Approved Group Inc., continues to make our vision a reality with her dedication and outstanding abilities (including her editing skills).

Åsa Nerelius and Mark Bourgeois, valued friends and amazing members of the Approved Group Inc. executive team, always impress me with their outstanding people skills and extra-mile resolve.

The incredibly talented team at Dexior Financial Inc., especially Gerard Darmon, Sai Jiwani Mohamed, Sanja Spasojevic, and Marc Poitras, gave their support and insight.

Our research team was relentless in their pursuit of the information this project required. Research coordinator Tanya Rauser spearheaded their efforts, spending countless hours contacting participants and organizing their responses. Researchers Paul Goudie, Clarice Abadilla, Vijay Anand, Jessica Andrews, Teresa Bailey, Mark Bourgeois, Joanna Bryniarska, Andrew Carson, Sean Cunningham, Shezmeen Hudani, Bianca Knop, Duncan Lea, Serena Lin, Jenna Lopez, Gordon Nesbitt, Don Roberts, Terri Rowson, Cassandra Stephens, and Frances Ubalde did an amazing job of cold-calling, interviewing, and collecting feedback from some of the busiest, hardest-to-reach decision-makers in North America.

My dedicated editorial team demanded excellence. Arlene Prunkl, Michelle Seidel, and Patricia Anderson, Ph.D., conducted the initial round of edits for the Business Development section, followed by Mitch Merker and Paul Goudie. Andy Fielding, chief editor of the Approved Series, did his usual outstanding job with the final edits and page design.

Mark Collins's foreword and David Scobey's introduction captured the spirit of the work we've done here, and emphasized its benefits for businesses and their customers.

Bob Kantin kindly allowed me to include an excerpt from his excellent book.

Dr. Stephen Grant, Ph.D., and countless other friends and associates, reviewed the Development section of this book at every stage and gave it the benefit of their objective opinions.

The Panel of Professional Purchasers shared their knowledge, experience, and unique perspectives.

Finally, my grandmother, Ruth Hannaford, my mother Angela Hannaford, and my nephew Ben Schell motivated me to stay focused on this project and see it through.

To all of you, my sincere thanks!

Foreword

More than ever, customers across North America are looking for real relationships. At Banknorth, we have done extensive research with our customers and found that they are looking for personalized service tailored to their needs as opposed to transaction-driven interactions.

Relationships require effective communication. That's why your business must continually listen to its customers. By creating new features and benefits inspired by customer feedback, your business can provide a distinctive buying experience and win a huge competitive advantage in the marketplace.

In today's competitive small-business environment, the proper alignment of sales, marketing, and training can be the difference between success and failure. *The Customer-Approved Small Business* presents this concept in a way that can benefit your business, whether it is new or established. Unlike other "how-to" books, this one is jam-packed with practical, usable ideas substantiated by careful research.

Most businesses deliver good levels of customer service, but today's customers require *excellent* service in exchange for their loyalty. To compete more effectively, small companies must not just meet, but exceed their customers' expectations.

When you consistently exceed your customers' expectations, they become a powerful sales force. It's a fact: The best way to get new business is through referrals from your existing customers.

As an energized advocate of this book, I wish you great success as you develop a business with satisfied, loyal customers and motivated, efficient staff.

– MARK COLLINS
EXECUTIVE VICE PRESIDENT OF MARKETING,
SALES STRATEGIES AND SMALL BUSINESS,
BANKNORTH GROUP INC.

Introduction

Small businesses are the growth engine of our economy. Not only are they an important source of financial strength, they provide entrepreneurs a path to pursue their dreams, and employees the chance to work in exciting and stretching environments. Small businesses are hard work, while at the same time rewarding and fun!

It is a well-known fact that many small businesses have a hard time succeeding. National statistics are as high as 60% failure during the first five years. *The Customer Approved Small Business* is certain to increase the success rate of any small business.

Based on research with those who matter most—small business customers—this book is packed with step-by-step ideas that help you:

- Communicate more effectively with your customers
- Collect important information from them to let you serve them better
- Offer solutions to their business problems
- Close sales

■ Grow your business

The foundation of the book is the Golden Rule: Treat your customers the way you want to be treated when you're the customer. It helps you better understand your customers' needs and enables you to better serve them. It helps you honor your customers by respecting and making good use of their time. It also helps you know your employees better and turn them into a real team—for their benefit, which ultimately benefits your business. There is no equal to this simple truth.

The book also stresses the importance of "measure twice, cut once"—which, when applied to your business, is "plan, plan, and then execute." This is an important and often overlooked business necessity. This is the only approach in business that will yield repeatable processes with predictable outcomes—the foundation for providing quality service to your customers. Abraham Lincoln captured this well when he said, "If I had eight hours to chop down a tree, I would spend six sharpening my axe."

We have used these same approaches to selling at BellSouth for many years, and know they really work. Large corporations have paid a lot more than $19.95 to learn, understand, and incorporate these selling methods into their businesses. This book is a real bargain and a must-read for every small and large business alike.

My best wishes to you as you incorporate these truths to differentiate yourself in the marketplace.

– David W. Scobey, Jr.
President
BellSouth Small Business Services

About This Book

Based on the proven Approved™ Series concept, *The Customer-Approved Small Business* is a practical, easy-to-use book that guides you, a small-business owner, through each step of business development and shows you how to build a solid foundation from which your business can grow.

To sell effectively, you must differentiate yourself from the competition. Some of the methods in this book require extra planning and preparation. If you're serious about competing in today's fast-paced business environment, you must be willing to put in this extra effort.

The Process

Our research team made thousands of phone calls and interviewed hundreds of corporate sales trainers, sales reps, and sales managers from companies across the U.S. to gather the most effective sales strategies used in corporate America today.

They then presented these strategies to purchasing professionals from over 200 companies across America for their ratings and comments.

- Total number of buyers: **228**
- Total number of interviews: **330**
- Total number of questions: **4,327**

The Buyers

We were fortunate to have such a tremendous group of professional buyers to contribute to this book. They had an average of over 17 years' experience, and many carried certifications including:

- Certified Purchasing Professional (CPP)
- Certified Professional Purchasing Manager (CPPM)
- Certified Purchasing Manager (C.P.M.)
- Accredited Purchasing Practitioner (A.P.P.)

The Companies

A wide variety of companies were surveyed: Smaller firms with 50 to 100 employees; major corporations (such as DaimlerChrysler, Oracle Corporation, Sara Lee, and Verizon) with thousands of employees; and companies in between. Industries included:

- Manufacturing
- Telecommunications
- Education
- Financial Services
- Aerospace
- Software
- Printing
- Health

- Hospitality
- Entertainment

Everything in this book is designed to help you create a business that is Customer-Approved. So enjoy the book, customize the Planning Guides, and live the success that comes from going the extra mile!

ONLINE RESOURCES

Planning Guides—You can download all of this book's Planning Guides as an Adobe Acrobat (PDF) file to print and customize for your business.

Survey Statistics—To keep this book's information easy-to-use, we have summarized the buyers' responses to our "What Did The Buyers Say?" survey questions. However, you are welcome to view the full statistical data for these surveys.

To access these resources, as well as periodic updates, special offers, and related information, please visit the special readers' webpage:

www.approvedseries.com/readers/tcasb/index.htm

---

x

Foundation

1

As a company adds new customers, additional stresses are put on it. This includes the possibility of overburdened, unprepared employees who can alienate customers.

Before you focus on developing more business, you must ensure that your company is operating efficiently and effectively. Only then can you confidently increase your customer base without worrying about how you will serve them.

This section will show you how to plan your business so you can be the kind of company that customers enjoy dealing with.

"**From my perspectives as a corporate purchaser** and a consumer, I always try to find companies that minimize my risk of making a poor or costly purchasing decision. If I'm treated differently each time I deal with a business, or if service or product quality is up and down, it makes me feel like anything can happen, and that's a risk. There are too many other companies for me to give my business to. Why should I deal with one that's all over the map?"

– CHRISTOPHER LOCKE
GLOBAL LEAD BUYER, DAIMLERCHRYSLER CORPORATION

Secret 1

Develop an operations manual

If you don't have an operations manual for your business, you need one. An operations manual documents, step-by-step, the one best way your employees should perform each repeatable process at your company. It is by far the best way your business can operate most efficiently and profitably.

An operations manual is not micro-management. It is a system that lets your staff do their best work by avoiding confusion and arbitrary decisions when performing routine processes. (Keep in mind that new situations and circumstances require decision-making—so don't make your operations manual so restrictive that it stifles appropriate employee creativity.)

Imagine if a national restaurant chain allowed the staff of each location to:

- Greet each customer however they wanted
- Decide whether or not to wash their hands before cooking
- Cook differently on each shift
- Decide when to open and close

If customers don't get consistency from a business, whose fault is it? Should your employees be allowed to make decisions on how to run your business and deal with your customers?

Of course not. Yet it happens all the time in small businesses—for example, when an owner leaves employees in charge who don't care if customers ever do business with them again. Ouch!

According to a study by Harvard Business School, the #1 reason that customers stop supporting a business is being treated with indifference by an employee. Let's see how you can help eliminate this threat to your business.

Standardize each process

To ensure a consistent experience for your employees and customers, you must standardize each process. This means selecting the best way to perform each process at your company—every time, no exceptions.

Q. How do you avoid exceptions?

A. You simply make the best way the rule. It becomes company policy. Your employees are taught to do their jobs by following the step-by-step instructions in your operations manual. Your operations manual is the essential tool that allows your business to run like clockwork—to the point where you could open ten new locations, and the staff at each would consistently know exactly what to do, when to do it, and how to do it.

The key: Remove the guesswork

A proper operations manual is designed to eliminate guesswork. Successful franchises have used this systemized approach for many years, and it has enabled them to greatly outperform less-structured independent businesses. However, there's no reason you can't use the same approach for your business too.

Sound complicated? It's not. As the saying goes, "The essence of brilliance is simplicity."

Unfortunately, people have a tendency to complicate things. That's why some companies end up employing amazingly inefficient methods.

Sometimes these businesses are lucky. A new employee arrives, sees an inefficient process, and says, "Have you tried doing it this way?", or, "Let me show you how we did it at my last job." Then the other employees watch in amazement as a complicated job becomes easy.

Then the boss hears about this new method and realizes that it could have saved his department thousands of dollars. So he calls everyone to a meeting and asks, "Why were you doing it the old way?"

"That's how we've always done it," the employees answer. Or they may say, "That's the way the person I replaced taught me. Then I taught the others . . ."

That's why you have no choice. You must systemize your business, and the way to do that is with a properly-designed operations manual. It takes some extra time and effort—but if you don't have that essential tool, and your company needs you 15 hours a day, you'll be on the way to burnout.

When you design a proper operations manual and get your business systemized, you:

- Free yourself from the tyranny of having to do everything yourself because no one else knows how.
- Allow your business to grow from a foundation of strength.
- Create a predictable experience for your employees and customers.
- Improve your employees' morale by giving them the tools they need to do their work as well as possible.
- Make your business more profitable.

- Make yourself feel like a real businessperson.

Also, when you document your processes, it's likely that you'll find ways to make them more efficient.

There are many books, seminars, and business courses on running your business efficiently and effectively. (A modern classic is *The E-myth Revisited: Why Most Small Businesses Don't Work, And What To Do About It* by Michael Gerber. Many business-owners consider it a "must-have.")

Secret 2

Hire self-starters who fit your team

Hiring the right people is the single most important—and challenging—task you will face as you start your business. There is no guarantee that the person you hire today will still be a good fit three months from now. However, there are steps you can take to minimize that risk.

Here is an example of a very successful recruiting and hiring system developed by Marketshare Research Institute for the position of telephone-based researcher. You can use a similar process to attract and identify the people fundamental to your success.

1. We set up a phone line to use as a dedicated job line. This job line is always answered by voice mail, never live.

2. We create and record an outgoing voice-mail message for the job line, which:

   a. States the position's requirements

   b. Briefly describes some benefits of working for the company

   c. Asks the applicant to provide the top two reasons why we should consider the applicant for an interview

   d. Thanks the applicant for calling

   e. Explains that, due to the high volume of calls received, only suitable applicants will be contacted

3. We place an ad in a newspaper or online job bank, showing the specific criteria for the position and the job line's phone number.

4. We review the messages on the job line and rate them on a scale from 1 to 10, based on quality of communication and message content. We then return only the calls that score 8 or better. Several people help in this process.

5. When we call the short-listed applicants, we ask them for 10 minutes for a telephone interview. We then ask some key questions we've created in advance. This gives us a sense of the applicant's ability to communicate spontaneously. (Effective communication is key to a successful business.)

6. When applicants pass Step 5, we invite them to our office for a brief interview. This gives us a better idea of their character, communication and people skills, work values, etc. We ask more questions which we've prepared in advance.

   If we're still impressed after this face-to-face meeting, we call the applicant again the following day to arrange the next step.

7. We hold a 30-minute informal meeting with the applicant and our staff. Yes, it takes time from our work, but nothing is more important than growing a company one quality person at a time. To justify this decision, we ask ourselves:

   Q. What is the cost of doing it?

   A. 30 minutes of the company's time.

   Q. What is the cost of *not* doing it?

   A. We run the risk of hiring someone who doesn't fit in with the rest of the team, resulting in lowered morale. If we train a new hire, then terminate them prior to our 90-day probation period, we have wasted time and money and are back to square one.

   Conclusion: It's worth the 30 minutes.

8. If the applicant seems like a good fit for our team, we give them one of our current corporate calling guides, and ask them to study it at home and do some role-play calls with a friend. This step is very helpful in identifying an applicant's work ethic and self-dis-

cipline. The applicants who follow through with this step are the kinds of self-starters we are likely to hire.

9. We arrange a two-day work trial, for which the applicant receives two days' normal wages. The trial:

   a. Shows us how well the applicant can do the required work

   b. Gives the applicant a chance to see if the job is right for them

   c. Gives our staff two days to get to know the applicant better—an important consideration

10. After the trial, our team votes on whether or not to hire the applicant. This encourages a team-based culture where everyone feels involved. If the applicant is accepted, we contact them the next day to offer the position.

Secret 3

Find the right people for outside sales

Many positions in a company are reactive (the receptionist, who answers the phone when it rings), and easy to measure (a production worker with a predetermined and measurable work flow).

By contrast, outside sales people must be proactive—self-starters who are motivated and determined to succeed with minimal supervision. Although they're usually required to do a certain amount of office work, outside sales people are generally allowed to manage their own time. This makes it crucial to choose the right people for the job.

Here are some questions you may find valuable when you interview outside sales applicants:

- Assuming we hire you, describe your activities during a typical day.
- How do you handle rejection?
- When it comes to making cold calls to companies to set appointments, what is your comfort level on a scale from 1 to 10, with 10 being most comfortable?
- How do you develop trust in a business relationship?
- What kind of system do you use to manage your time?
- How do you prioritize your task list?

"**Far too many times,** I've tried to do business with employees who made me feel I was simply 'in the way'. I'm not just referring to retail, but to various businesses—including some well-known ones I won't mention. It's insulting to be treated with a total lack of respect, and the company-owners and management should know better. Needless to say, when I'm treated like that, I never go back."

– A TOUGH CUSTOMER

Secret 4

Keep only the right people on your team

Employees can make or break your company—so when you evaluate job candidates, it's crucial to focus on important qualities including character, communication skills, people skills, and work ethic.

Even with effective hiring systems, however, people can change. So can your company's goals. You may find that some employees, no matter how carefully they were originally chosen, are no longer a good fit for your needs.

Despite the danger of retaining these employees, some business-owners find reasons to avoid firing them. They may find the firing process too stressful or distasteful, or they may personally like employees who are clearly no longer appropriate. So they let the employees stay and hope things change for the better. When they don't, frustration sets in and the company is weakened.

Mediocrity is not acceptable

Here is the bottom line: You, as a business-owner, are not responsible for any employee's need for a job. To succeed in today's extremely-competitive business world, you must repeat this mantra: "Mediocrity is not acceptable." It is simply not possible, or fair, to put an employee's needs ahead of those of your business and your customers.

It's not the people you let go who hurt your business. It's the ones you know you should let go—and don't.

So make a concerted effort to hire as wisely as possible. Take your time, and don't hire someone hastily just to meet the demands of production. View each new hire as one of the most important decisions you make, and you will have a huge advantage. However, if an employee is no longer an asset to your business, you must allow someone more appropriate to take their place.

An extra secret for keeping the right employees

Once you've found the people that can help you grow your business, it's important to keep them happy and motivated to stay with you. One of the best things you can do is to include your team in key decisions and changes. The feeling of having one's opinions valued and solicited is vital to job satisfaction, yet far too many companies and managers ignore this basic need. It can't be stressed enough.

Secret 5

Develop an employee manual

An employee manual (a separate document from your operations manual) is a key element of a proper business—yet a stunning majority of small businesses never make the time or effort to develop one. Even if you have only two employees, it's still a necessity.

Designing your own employee manual is not as difficult as you may think. Many excellent templates are available. (Take a look at www.bizmanuals.com for some examples). Once you've completed your manual, you'll find it helps your business immeasurably and makes your employees feel like they matter.

At Approved Publications, our employee manual includes our company's history. We update it regularly and are sure to include all new key events. Our manual gets a lot of positive feedback from new hires. People like to know about the company they work for, and every company has a story!

Key benefits of an employee manual:

- It protects your business from potential lawsuits by having employees sign off on the rules that govern your business (such as those concerning termination), provided these rules are clearly-defined and within the employment standards governing your area.

- Along with your operations manual, it makes your company's policies and requirements black-and-white, eliminating the destructive gray zone that inevitably creates problems that can harm your business.

- It helps you define in advance your company's personality and culture, describing such things as dress codes, holiday pay, and how many times an employee can be late before receiving a verbal or written warning.

Secret 6

Create a job description for each position

Want focused employees with a clear sense of purpose who feel good about their daily contributions to the company's goals? Then be sure you have clearly-defined job descriptions for each position in your business (including your own).

Be sure to share the job descriptions of the various positions with your team. It's important for everyone to understand who is responsible for specific tasks and duties.

That said, you must also be sure to assign and train backup people to cover the tasks and duties of each position in case the primary person is absent or on vacation. Never get stuck in this kind of trap: "Only Rhonda knows how to do that, and she's out of town till Thursday . . ."

Clearly-defined job descriptions create a more positive corporate culture, which helps increase overall productivity and quality of work. Most people appreciate and work better with structure and predictability in their work life. Include regularly-scheduled employee reviews (also called "performance evaluations"), and watch your productivity soar.

If you don't define your expectations in advance, you can create an environment of frustration and confusion, as employees start making assumptions about who does what. It's one thing to hire someone and tell them what their responsibilities and duties are. But if they arbitrarily receive extra duties as time goes on, they can become resentful, thinking, "I wasn't hired to do that . . ."

Write a proper business plan

Secret 7

Many business-owners underestimate the amounts of money and time it will take to make their businesses profitable. One of the top reasons businesses fail is undercapitalization—when the money runs out before the business can begin to sustain itself.

When you look for financing, a business plan is an absolute necessity. But even if you have no immediate financing requirements, you need a dynamic, fluid, evolving business plan as a roadmap to profitability.

Writing a business plan can be hard, time-consuming work. But so is university, technical school, or any other commitment to excellence. This is your business, and your life! It's essential that you take the time to prepare your plan. It will give you a sense of clarity and focus, and you'll feel like a true business-owner.

Key benefits of a business plan:

- Clearly defines your business goals and objectives
- Vital for obtaining funding
- Lets you determine where to focus your business resources
- Helps you identify your strengths and weaknesses

Many helpful, time-saving business-plan templates are available on the Internet. Palo Alto Software's Business Plan Pro (`www.businessplanpro.com`) is an excellent resource, containing templates for many types of businesses.

On the next page, you'll see a suggested outline for creating your own business plan.

Example: Business plan outline

- Title Page
- Table of Contents
- Executive Summary
- Vision and Mission
- Objectives
- Company Overview
- Management
- Product / Service Strategy
- Market Analysis
- Marketing Plan
- Financial Projections

Banks and credit unions are always happy to provide financing to credit-approved business owners with a viable, well-thought-out business plan. Most institutions also provide information resources to help their small-business clients.

If traditional sources of business capital elude you, other options are venture capital firms or private investment banks. These firms usually provide capital in exchange for equity or part ownership in your business. An example of a private investment bank is Dexior Financial Inc. (www.dexior.com). As well as capital, they provide their partner companies with valuable management expertise and assistance in key areas like taxation, bookkeeping, marketing, and legal.

Other potential sources of capital are U.S. government grants. 26 federal grant agencies and over 900 individual grant programs award $350 *billion* in business grants each year. It's worth a visit to www.grants.gov/index to see if your business qualifies for any of them.

Developing New Business

2

The ability of your small business to survive and prosper almost certainly depends on the number of contacts you can make with the companies you target, and how you and your representatives conduct yourselves during those contacts.

For this reason, this next section will show you proven, proactive strategies to positively influence the decision-makers you approach, and what to do when you communicate with them.

Marketing comprises a wide range of activities, including:

- Market research
- The Internet
- Strategic alliances
- Analyzing the competition
- Positioning and pricing your products and services
- Direct mail
- Public relations
- Advertising campaigns

However, many small businesses don't have the resources to regularly use the more costly marketing methods.

Many small-business owners think that unsolicited direct-mail marketing will pay off for them. I remember a friend with an attractive and reputable business offer. His product was in demand and had already proven itself. He paid a princely sum for a mailing list of 15,000 decision-makers in his target market. He paid another large sum to produce an excellent marketing package which included a trial version of his CD-ROM.

He mailed the 15,000 packages to his target list at enormous expense to his small business. Guess how many sales he generated? Zero. How many responses and inquiries did he receive? Zero.

I'm happy to report that in spite of his lost capital, my friend went on to do amazingly well with his business—and he has not resorted to unsolicited direct mail again.

I know of many other direct-mail fiascos, but I won't bore you with the details. There are exceptions to everything, of course, but I would not feel good about myself if I recommended unsolicited direct mail in this book.

TV, newspaper, and magazine ads won't be covered here either. If you have the money required to produce an effective ad campaign and run it with the frequency required to get results, you'll likely be working with an advertising agency and be in the hands of experts.

The approaches I recommend here are approaches that most small businesses can afford—and they work. I know this from my own experience, and the experiences of many others who use them.

The system you'll learn here will enable you to generate new customers professionally and proactively. You'll be able to compete for business from larger, recognized companies. Once you start gaining these "name-brand" customers, you can leverage them for further growth: Other companies will be more willing to place their faith and trust in you, and your sales process will become easier and easier.

The sales methods we introduce in this section cover all stages of the sales process. They're based on interviews with hundreds of experienced buyers from a variety of industries. They were initially produced for the Approved Series title, *Buyer-Approved Selling: Sales Secrets from the Buyer's Side of the Desk*. Because these methods are recommended by actual buyers, you can use them with confidence—and that makes a big difference.

The heart of effective sales

As your business grows, it's likely that your sales team will grow, freeing you to focus on executive duties. However, as the owner of a small business—especially a new one—you have probably spent at least part of your time as a sales person.

Q. Do I need a specific type of personality to be good at sales?

A. No! Being a good sales person is more about character, work ethic, and proper training than personality. If you want to make good impressions in your business dealings, you need to build trust, use effective communication techniques, and—very importantly—show that you do not waste decision-makers' time. We will cover these key points in detail.

Here's some more good news: The great majority of businesspeople and sales people do *not* use the Customer-Approved secrets described in the next section with any consistency! When you use them, you'll have a distinct competitive advantage and earn more business.

Getting your prospect database in order

Many companies specialize in providing databases of corporate and residential prospects with specific contact information. Companies that sell contact data either compile and sell it themselves or sell databases produced by others.

This book focuses on B2B sales, so we will examine corporate databases. For each prospect, these databases can include:

- Company name
- Phone number
- Address
- Names and titles of key personnel (President, VP of Marketing, etc.)
- Years in business
- Annual revenue
- Number of employees
- Other pertinent data

List-brokers can create targeted lists according to your specific needs.

Example 1: Prospect Database

Let's assume that your key prospecting targets are vice presidents of operations for the largest California-based electronics manufacturers. You can have a list-broker such as **infoUSA** generate a database using the following criteria:

- **Industry** (or SIC code): Electronic manufacturers (all types)
- **Contact title**: Vice presidents of operations

- **Location**: California
- **Number of employees**: 250+
- **Annual revenue:** $50 million+
- **Years in business**: [All]

Example 2: Prospect Database

Your targets are the same as above, but include smaller companies as well:

- **Industry (or SIC code)**: Electronic manufacturers (all types)
- **Contact title**: Vice presidents of operations
- **Location**: California
- **Number of employees**: 20-250
- **Annual revenue**: $5-50 million
- **Years in business**: 5+

As you can see, you can be quite specific.

Q. How is the data delivered to me?

A. Data from infoUSA is available via email or on CD in Microsoft Excel spreadsheet format. It's easy to import the Excel data into the contact management software of your choice. (We'll discuss those software options shortly.)

Q. How accurate is the data from list-brokers?

A. For the most part, very accurate. infoUSA offers accuracy of 95% for phone numbers and addresses. Due to the changing nature of the business world, however, some data, such as employee names and titles, may need updating.

Challenges with data

There is one important challenge in generating corporate contact records: Most high-profile companies are relentlessly targeted by sales calls, so some of these companies request that their information be excluded from targeted searches.

This means that you could request a search in a specific industry and city, and the high-profile companies you'd expect to see might not be included. This doesn't mean they are not listed in the database; it just means that the list-broker cannot find their records unless the broker keys in exact company names. This is a significant constraint you should be aware of.

Q. How do I find these high-profile companies that may be excluded?

A. One way is to use a free online service such as `www.yellowpages.com` and simply enter the city name and business category you are targeting.

Another option are the local Business Journals published by American City Business Journals (`www.bizjournals.com`).

If your target city is covered by one of the 62 Business Journals published in key US markets, you can buy their book of lists. They are updated annually and provide data, key facts, and contact information for thousands of top local businesses, industries, professions, governmental units, and non-profit organizations in each city.

Organizing your prospect database for maximum results

To maximize the return on your selling efforts, it's vital that you have a systemized approach to bringing in new business.

You may already have a strategy for managing and prioritizing your prospect database, but if you don't, you'll benefit by implementing this systematic approach to effective prospecting:

1. Compile or create your total prospect list.

2. Prioritize and number your list according to each prospect's potential. If you are using data from a list-broker, you will have information on each prospect's number of employees and annual revenue to help you identify their potential.

3. From this master list, create a new list for each industry type. Since you have numbered your original list in the order of each prospect's potential, your new vertical-market lists will also be in that order.

4. Identify and prioritize the vertical markets or industry types that are the easiest to sell to or who stand to benefit the most from your product or service.

Now that you have an organized list of prospects, you have a choice: You can call the most promising ones first, or you can "practice" your sales approach on the least-promising ones and work your way to the top of the list. If you're new to the art of selling, the second approach is a great way to get your feet wet.

Q. Now that I have my list organized, how do I manage it?

A. Depending on your specific needs, a variety of contact-management software is available. You can conduct and track your prospecting activities much more efficiently with a computer-based contact-manager than with an old-fashioned paper-based system. Consider some of the things you will need to manage:

- Calling the right person back at the right number when you said you would

- Sending specific information when you said you would

- Following up on the information you've sent, when you said you would

- Preparing and personally delivering or couriering proposals when you said you would

23

You have enough challenges running your business. You don't need the extra challenge of trying to juggle all this information (and more) on a million pieces of paper! If you don't use a computer-based contact-manager, you can bet your competition is using one—so it's in your best interest to do so too. Some good contact-managers include:

- ACT!
- Maximizer
- GoldMine

Which one you use is a matter of personal choice. Some have trial versions you can download from the developer's website so you can see which best suits your needs. Used properly, these systems will increase your productivity and keep you on-track. You won't know how you got along without one.

Secret 9

(Crucial!)

Don't call the contacts in your database until you've read and customized Secrets 10-14

Once you've organized your contacts, the most effective way to sell to them is to phone them and set face-to-face appointments. Phoning prospects you don't know (known as "cold-calling") can seem daunting—unless you use the methods that follow.

Some or all of your prospects may be outside your local area, and it may not be practical to meet with them in person. In such cases, some businesses make the mistake of calling prospects and attempting to do their entire sales presentations right then and there.

Instead, use the methods we describe to set telephone appointments with your prospects. This:

- Shows respect for your prospects' time by letting them arrange appointments that fit their schedules
- Makes it more likely that your (less-stressed) prospects will be receptive to your presentation
- Makes you look confident and professional

Secrets 10-14 will guide you through an effective and proven process that will enable you to call your prospects with confidence.

"I get irritated when a rep doesn't understand the products they are selling and the applications of that product. This happens far too often . . . The problem seems to be that companies hire good salespeople but not good industry-specific people."

– JIM MOREY, VICE PRESIDENT OF PROCUREMENT
SARA LEE FOODS, A DIVISION OF SARA LEE CORPORATION

Create an Industry-Specific Positioning Statement (ISPS)

Secret 10

It's likely that your business sells to different vertical markets or industries. If so, you'll be well advised to develop your own customized ISPS—a concise statement of what you do and your potential benefit to your prospect. The buyers we interviewed agreed that an ISPS positively influenced the way they perceived a business. You never get a second chance to make a first impression, so developing your own ISPS is time well-spent.

To lay the groundwork for your ISPS, and for your sales efforts in general, it's important to do your homework. Become a specialist in your industry. Learn about its technologies, challenges, and marketing trends. Learn the industry's vernacular. People prefer to deal with experts who understand their industry's needs and challenges. Nothing is more frustrating, or less impressive, than dealing with a supplier who doesn't know the field they serve.

When you introduce your company on a first phone call or in a first meeting, your ISPS helps stimulate your prospect's interest and curiosity. It introduces you as an industry specialist, and tells the prospect that you can increase revenues or reduce costs. It's a sentence that crystallizes the main benefits of doing business with you.

Think of other business-owners you know. How many of them can express the essence of their businesses in a single well-constructed sentence?

ISPS Examples

1. You sell inventory-management software to the electronics-manufacturing industry:

    ISPS: "We specialize in lowering inventory-management costs for electronics manufacturers."

2. You provide lead lead-generation services to universities, colleges, and other businesses who seek to increase revenue through higher enrollment. When targeting the educational sector you could say:

    ISPS: "We're enrollment-creation specialists for the educational industry."

3. You sell corporate travel services, and you have several accounts in the financial-services industry:

    ISPS (for targeting the financial-services industry): "We specialize in saving financial institutions time and money on their travel arrangements."

Planning Guide: Creating an ISPS

Step 1: Using the lists you made in Step 3 of Secret 8 *(see pg. 23)*, create a list of companies you want to target.

Step 2: Identify and learn the industry vernacular while researching each company's website. Write down key words and phrases for potential use in your ISPS.

Step 3: Find out which associations serve the industry and write their names here. Research their websites and publications to understand the current state of that vertical market.

Step 4: Identify the key benefits your product or service offers this market.

Step 5: Write your ISPS.

- Try to limit your ISPS to 15 words. Remember, your objective is to quickly determine a potential fit with your prospect.

- Emphasize how you can increase revenues or decrease expenses.

- Become so familiar with your ISPS that it is second-nature to you. You never know when you may meet a potential customer. It's to your advantage to be able to concisely describe your business without having to stop and think about it.

- Use language your customer cares about and understands.

The Buyers Comment: ISPS

"Excellent approach. The key here is to increase your knowledge—not to learn new buzzwords for selling, but a real, honest-to-goodness knowledge base you can apply to the customer's industry-specific needs. Surface knowledge will get you in the door, but having a real working knowledge of the processes, requirements, and solutions will keep you there!"

– WM. FRANK QUIETT, C.P.M., A.P.P.
PROJECT LEAD, SUPPLY CHAIN MANAGEMENT AND STRATEGIC SOURCING

"There is nothing more irritating than someone who doesn't understand the pressures specific to my industry . . . This approach is an excellent way for a sales rep to learn about our business and be prepared."

– ERIK SCHLICHTING
INVENTORY CONTROL MANAGER

"I get calls all the time and the salespeople seem to either patronize or fumble. If they knew what my company did, and knew more about our industry, they would be smoother and much less annoying. I don't think I should have to teach them how to sell to my industry."

– JUDY ELRITE, C.P.M.
BUYER SPECIALIST

"About 50% of my suppliers use this approach. The other 50% tend to focus on their company history and prior accomplishments rather than the benefits and opportunities for the client. They talk about their company instead of mine."

– CHRISTOPHER LOCKE
GLOBAL LEAD BUYER
DAIMLERCHRYSLER CORPORATION

Secret 11

Design a Primary Reason Statement (PRS)

If you have never sold to a particular industry, an ISPS won't work for you. You can't validly claim experience in that particular field. In such cases, use a Primary Reason Statement (PRS).

If you serve many industries, it can actually be to your advantage not to give the impression that you exclusively serve one industry. For example, if you make bookkeeping software, it may be to your advantage to give the impression that businesses find your product versatile and easy to use, regardless of their specialties.

A PRS is a single sentence that identifies your line of business and tells your prospect the primary reason that companies *in any field* do business with you. Structure your PRS by combining your line of business with the word "specialists" or "specialize" to highlight your company's ability to increase revenues or decrease expenses in a specific area.

Examples: Primary Reason Statement

- "We're a corporate travel agent, and we specialize in reducing the time and money companies spend on business travel."

- "We're a software company, and we specialize in lowering inventory-management costs."

Secret 12

Create some Key Point Statements (KPS)

Buyers tell us that they hear a lot of long-winded reasons why they should set appointments with cold-calling businesspeople. Clearly those people have not taken the time to create and rehearse short, clearly-articulated statements of the key reasons buyers do business with them.

Key Point Statements deliver clear, concise information about your company/product/service—especially when you have limited time to get your point across and need to make a quick impact.

Two well-written Key Point Statements that can be given in 15 seconds or less can be very effective—not only for cold calls, but in chance encounters with prospects (so-called "elevator speeches").

Remember, Key Point Statements are not sales presentations, so keep them brief. (We will incorporate your Key Point Statements in the Permission-Based Cold Call Guide in Secret 13 *[page 33]*.)

Example: Key Point Statements

For this example, we'll imagine your company sells travel services to businesses.

Step 1: List the four key points you want to make during the call.

- Your customers include Fortune 1000 companies.
- You provide the highest level of personal service in the industry.
- You provide the lowest airfare and hotel rates in North America.
- You're experts at making last-minute arrangements.

Step 2: Use any two key points from your list in Step 1 to create your two Key Point Statements:

- "We provide the lowest airfare and hotel rates in North America, and we're experts at making last-minute arrangements."
- "We offer the highest level of personal service in the industry, and we work for a number of Fortune 1000 clients."

Planning Guide: Key Point Statements

Step 1: Identify the four key points you will use in your Key Point Statements.

Step 2: Use the two points that go together best to create the first Key Point Statement.

Step 3: Combine the remaining two to form your second statement.

"I prefer to be asked for a moment of my time, but only about 20% of sales reps ever do that."

— Lori Patten, Director of Projects–Development
Hyatt Hotels Corporation

"Most of the reps who call on me don't ask permission for my time. When they do ask, and I don't have time, I usually show my appreciation by trying to schedule a future call."

— Tina M. Lowenthal, Associate Director
Purchasing Services, California Institute of Technology

The Permission-Based Cold Call Guide

As we've discussed, your first call to your prospect has one goal: setting a qualified appointment. If you've completed the steps in Secrets 10 through 12, it's simple to customize your own calling guide using the Customer-Approved permission-based cold call model.

Secret 13

Some sales trainers think you should open cold calls by immediately delivering a key benefit, without first asking for a moment of the prospect's time. They believe that asking permission gives the prospect a chance to shut down the call before it begins.

However, could this lack of courtesy start you off on the wrong foot, and make you seem invasive and annoying? The answer is *yes*.

Marketshare Research Institute has used a permission-based approach in over 150,000 cold calls to prospects in over 100 cities across America, in a variety of industries, including:

- Accounting

- Software
- Higher education
- Business associations
- Professional Sports
- Financial services
- Office equipment
- Corporate training

An impressive 85% of the prospects responded favorably and agreed to proceed with the call. Of the remaining 15%, the vast majority simply asked to be called again at a more convenient time. Using permission-based call models, Marketshare Research Institute has set over 8000 appointments with busy decision-makers across America. These statistics indicate that you should feel confident using this model, regardless of your business type or location.

Use the model below to create your own permission-based guide for seeking appointments. This model assumes you have identified the decision-maker for your products or services.

1. Ask for permission to open the call

"Hi, Monica, this is Cassandra from ABC Co. I don't need much time—do you have a quick minute?"

2. Present your ISPS or PRS

"Thanks, Monica. We specialize in saving financial institutions time and money on their travel arrangements."

3. Determine the prospect's level of knowledge of your company and product or service

"Are you familiar with / have you ever used / do you know much about [choose one]:

- ... our company?"
- ... this process?"
- ... this type of service?"
- ... this product?"
- ... this kind of application?"

4. Ask for permission to present your Key Point Statements

"Is it okay if I tell you a couple of key points about [choose one]:

- ... us?"
- ... what we do?"
- ... our product?"
- ... this process?"

5. Present your Key Point Statements

"We provide the lowest airfare and hotel rates in North America, and we're experts at making last-minute arrangements."

"We offer the highest level of personal service in the industry, and we do work for a number of Fortune 1000 clients."

6. Ask your qualifying question

"Monica, I have a quick question for you: Based on what I've told you so far, can you see any potential for ABC Co. to be of value to your business, either now or at some point down the road?"

7. Ask for the appointment

"Monica, it would be great if I could stop by to see if we can help you out in any way. Are you available next Thursday? I won't waste your time."

[Prospect] Yes, I'll be here.

"Great—would 10:30 work for you?"

[Prospect] No, I'm in meetings until noon.

"Okay, how about 3 P.M.?"

8. Confirm the appointment

"Perfect. Just to confirm, then: I'll meet you at your office, 1070 Main Street, at 3 P.M. on Thursday, June the first. Did I get that right?"

[Prospect] Yes.

"Monica, may I leave my contact details with you?"

[You leave your name and number]

"Thanks Monica, I'll see you next Thursday."

Supplements to the Permission-Based Cold Call model

1. When they don't have a "quick minute"

When you ask, "Do you have a quick minute?", your prospect may say, "No, it's not a good time." Marketshare's experience suggests that this response is most effective:

"Is it okay if I give you a call back some other time?"

[Prospect] Yes, that's fine.

"Thanks. When would be the best time for me to call you back?"

2. When they just want information

One common response during a cold call is, "Can you just send me some information?" To effectively handle this question, consider these responses:

"Monica, I could send information, but in the interest of saving your time, how's this? I've developed a 10-minute meeting *(see pg. 40)* designed to identify our potential value to you. 10 minutes and I'm out the door. I won't waste your time."

If the prospect declines:

"Shall I email you a link to our website, or do you prefer printed information in the mail?"

[Prospect replies]

"Okay, I'll get that out to you today. May I give you a quick call next Friday to see if a meeting makes sense for you then?"

"Using voice mail to leave a message or sales pitch is meaningless without personal interaction. People are tired of machine-to-machine voice tag. Make the effort to contact them personally."

– WM. FRANK QUIETT, C.P.M., A.P.P., PROJECT LEAD
SUPPLY CHAIN MANAGEMENT AND STRATEGIC SOURCING

Don't leave voice mail on cold calls

Imagine you're a buyer. How likely is it that you'll have the time to return a continual barrage of unsolicited voice mail from businesspeople you don't know, selling things you may not even need? Is that an effective way to initiate contact with a prospect?

Secret 14

The Buyers Comment: Cold-call voice mail

"No, I don't like voice mail for initial contact. Sales reps should try again until they get through."

– DON WALRAVEN
DIRECTOR OF INVENTORY MANAGEMENT
ALASKA DISTRIBUTORS CO.

"It's better for a salesperson to keep calling until they get hold of me. It's in their best interest to do so, since in most cases, I'm busy and may have to delete the message and move on."

– GREG ADKINS
PURCHASING MANAGER

"No, I very seldom return voice mail from reps who are prospecting. If I did that,

I would be calling forty people a day. Is there a better way? Call until I answer the phone."

– Paula L. Martin
Corporate IT Buyer

"**A 10-minute meeting** is a very ambitious objective. That promise may get you in the door—*once*. To ensure you are on the road to building a partnership, you must accomplish what you have promised. You should work to stay on track, keep focused on the points you wish to make, and close your presentation with opportunities for cost-reduction. In today's economy, more and more buyers are operating under a cost reduction charter from upper management. If you can help them achieve this goal, they will be more likely to listen and be open to further discussions."

– LYNNE E. GEHRKE
VICE PRESIDENT, PROCUREMENT, A. B. DICK COMPANY

The 10-Minute Meeting

Secret 15

When you're a buyer with limited time, choosing the sales reps you deal with is a matter of risk and reward. Businesspeople who waste a buyer's time with unprepared, unstructured meetings fall into the high-risk category, no matter how charming and likable they may be. Times have changed, and most of the buyers we spoke to agreed: The days of socializing sales calls are over.

Decision-makers constantly get calls for first-time appointments with new suppliers of products and services. If a busy decision maker meets with only two new businesspeople a week, that adds up to 100 new meetings in a year.

Most sales books teach that people buy only from people they like and trust, so it's no wonder that many suppliers spend the first 10 minutes of their initial meetings on unnecessary "relationship-building" small talk. But what do busy decision-makers think about this? Do they really want small talk? According to our research, the answer is *no*.

Our research shows that buyers prefer dealing with businesspeople who respect their limited time. The best way to do this is to state, up-front, that you have prepared a structured meeting with the objective of determining if you can offer the buyer a benefit that merits further discussion at the buyer's convenience.

Consider this approach:

"Monica, I know you're busy. I've prepared a 10-minute meeting agenda that will quickly determine if our company can be of value to you. When could we meet for 10 minutes? I guarantee I won't waste your time."

To prepare for an effective 10-minute meeting:

- Research the prospect's company.
- Define your meeting objective.
- Prepare and rehearse a brief overview of your company.
- Prepare intelligent, insightful questions.
- Rehearse your 10-minute power meeting.

It's amazing what you can accomplish in 10 minutes when you stay focused. Let's assume you employ the 10-minute meeting, and it leads to an ongoing business relationship. Continuing to set brief, structured meetings is a good way to maintain the relationship. You avoid being perceived as a risk to the buyer's limited time. The buyer is more likely to retain your company as a supplier, and—very importantly—to feel confident referring you to others.

Note: In Secret 23 *(pg. 63)*, we introduce the Advance Meeting Agenda (AMA). With an initial 10-minute meeting, you've already stated your objective, so an AMA is not required.

The Buyers Comment: The 10-Minute Meeting

"This approach shows respect for my time. Also, when a busy buyer is swamped with back-to-back meetings, this allows 5 or 10 minutes in between to check phone messages etc. It is not pleasant to be escorting someone out of the office while another one waits."

– YVONNE VENTIMIGLIA
DIVISION MANAGER, LEVERAGE PURCHASING
LAYNE CHRISTENSEN COMPANY

"Time is valuable, so I think it's a great idea!"

–PAULA L. MARTIN
CORPORATE IT BUYER

"Yes, I believe a power meeting can be a good door-opener."

– WENDY IMAMURA, C.P.M., CPPB, CMIR
MATERIAL PROCESSING CENTER MANAGER
VERIZON HAWAII INC.

"There's a really good chance that I would read a postcard versus a letter. Postcards are easier to read and they quickly identify any key points. I think that this is a very effective method of direct mail."

– Henry Valiulus, Director of Purchasing

Customized business postcards

Imagine this scenario: You've spoken with a prospect and determined they may need your product or service–not immediately, but in the future.

Secret 16

While it's important to maintain contact, the buyers we spoke with unanimously agreed that there was a fine line between keeping in touch with your prospects and annoying them. After three or four months of check-in calls, a call every month may cease to be effective and become unwelcome.

This presents you with a dilemma:

- Excessive follow up—annoy the buyer and lose the sale
- Not enough follow up—be forgotten and lose the sale

In situations like this, a creative or humorous postcard can be effective. Using them to supplement your follow-up calls may increase your chances of getting business when the prospect is ready to buy.

Example: Custom postcard

A few years ago, Approved Publications needed a short-run printing of books, so we requested quotes from several suppliers. The proposals were followed up by calls, but by that time, our plans had been delayed. The only thing we could tell the reps was that we didn't know when we would need to run the job.

Four months later, we unexpectedly received an eye-catching postcard promoting short-run printing technology. It had a picture of a forlorn-looking author slumped at her desk, surrounded by thousands of copies of her new book. The caption read, "Why hasn't Oprah called?"

This card caught our attention. Its timing was impeccable, too, as we were now ready to go to print.

To create your own business postcard, all you need is an idea that shows your product or service solving a problem—or, as with the card in the example, an idea showing the consequences of not using your product or service. You can also use postcards to communicate your Industry Specific Positioning Statement *(pg. 26)*.

What Did The Buyers Say?

from Marketshare Research Institute

The buyers we surveyed said that **only 14% of reps** used customized business postcards.

(Average of responses)

The Buyers Comment: Custom business postcards

"I would probably read a postcard as they are usually more to the point. If it is of interest, then I would follow up and ask for more literature."

– Peter Van der Hoek
Buyer/Planner

"If it is not addressed directly to me, it goes straight to the trash. Be sure the mailing is addressed specifically to the person you wish to reach. Items addressed 'Attn: Purchasing Dept.' or 'Attn: Purchasing Mgr.' probably won't reach anyone. Many places have instructions in their mail-sorting areas to dispose of that type of mail immediately."

– Richard K. Tyler, C.P.M.
Director of Purchasing
MRC Bearings

"I would look at it, if it were an interesting postcard. What I would really like to see is a postcard that incorporated a business card, with perforations to remove the card for future reference."

– Brad Bigelow
Manager of Purchasing and Vendor Relations

Don't meet with a buyer or decision-maker until you've completed Secrets 18-27!

Secret 17

(Crucial!)

In some ways, setting an appointment with a buyer or other decision-maker is similar to winning a role in a stage play or movie. Just as you would never go on stage without proper preparation and rehearsal, you should never go to a sales meeting and "wing it." Only the confidence borne of preparation will allow you to maximize your opportunity and dramatically increase your chance of out-performing the competition.

Even if the person you're meeting with can't authorize the funds for your product or service, it's important to remember that they probably have the power to say "no." It's vital to make a good first impression.

As with most of the Customer-Approved methods we describe, it's amazing that most businesspeople neglect to use these during first meetings—and that's good news for you! It's your chance to differentiate yourself from your competition and earn more business.

"Credibility dissipates in front of your eyes. I won't trust their business and they won't get my business."

– Wayne Nordin C.P.M.
V.P. & Procurement Manager, Sun Trust Bank

Secret 18

Pre-meeting research

Too many businesspeople arrive at first meetings with questions they could have answered with the most basic research! Don't waste your prospect's time—do your homework. The business professionals who win key accounts usually do extensive research before meeting with prospects. Your prospects may not always notice that you've done this extra research, but they'll sure notice when you haven't!

Here are some questions you may want to answer before the meeting:

- How many locations do they have, and is this the head office?
- Is the company private or public, and is there a parent company?
- Have they or are they acquiring any companies?
- Have they recently been in the news or had other major publicity?
- Who are their competitors?
- Who are their major customers?
- Why do their customers buy from them?
- What is their annual revenue?
- When is their fiscal year-end?
- What are their main product or service lines?
- Has anyone in senior management recently been replaced?

- Are they in a budget freeze?
- What are their major challenges?

To help with your research, try Web-search tools such as Google (`www.google.com`) or Copernic (`www.copernic.com`). For publicly-traded companies, try Yahoo Finance (`http://finance.yahoo.com/`), where you can find financial information, employee counts, officers' names, and website links. For business statistics and resources, try BizStats.Com (`www.bizstats.com`).

What Did The Buyers Say?

from Marketshare Research Institute

The buyers we surveyed said that prior research
by reps rated **8.13 out of 10** in importance.

They said that **only 49.9% of reps** seemed
to do research prior to their initial meetings.

(Averages of responses)

The Buyers Comment: Pre-meeting research

"I do not do business with someone who has not taken the time to know about my business."

– Sheryl Haeberle
Buyer, Brigham Young University

"I generally turn them off quickly and terminate the meeting."

– Jim Haining, C.P.M., A.P.P., MBA
Manager, Corporate Agreements
for a leading telecommunications company

"It's a big negative if someone comes to a first meeting with me without doing proper research on my company. They've wasted my time, as I've probably had to explain things they could have found out about us in the public domain."

– Mike Kanze, MBA, C.P.M., A.P.P.
President, Cornerstone Services Incorporated

"It is rare for someone else to raise the objection first. It's unusual, but it's a very good idea."

– BRIAN SMITH
DIRECTOR OF INVENTORY MANAGEMENT, CORPORATE EXPRESS

Create some Genuine Preemptive Objection Statements (GPOS)

Secret 19

Does this sound familiar?: You're making a presentation, and it's going well—until your prospect raises an objection. Suddenly, your carefully-organized presentation has taken a 45-degree turn, and you're on the defensive.

It doesn't have to be that way. When you can *anticipate* your prospect's objections and address them in a positive and informative way, you can actually give your prospect some key insights and enhance your presentation.

That's the power of the Genuine Preemptive Objection Statement (GPOS). We emphasize the word "genuine"—a GPOS works only when it is logical and forthright.

For example, if the conversation turns to price, you can introduce the following GPOS before your prospect brings up a lower-priced competitor:

"Yes, let's talk about price for a moment. Our product/service is priced about 20% higher than most of our competitors'—yet we're signing new business all the time.

"The reason people buy from us is value. You see, independent research confirms our product's lifespan is nearly double the industry standard. So you get double the value, yet you pay only 20% more."

Notice how the businessperson cited his company's high standards without directly criticizing the competition. This is part of the "positive" in GPOS; it shows confidence and integrity.

In this next example, your company is a small service provider. Your prospect has just complained about frequent service interruptions with their current provider. The prospect's next thought could be, "If XYZ MegaCorp can't give us dependable service, how can you?" This is a chance to use a GPOS.

You can preempt the objection by explaining that your company's smaller size is what allows you to specialize and provide better service than a larger, diversified company:

"John, we're one of the smallest providers in the city, so it made sense for us to focus on a particular market niche and become experts in it. That's allowed us to deliver 23% more up-time than the local industry average."

Once you become familiar with the GPOS concept, you will realize there are regular opportunities to use them in prospect meetings. The key is to have your GPOS rehearsed and ready, so you can notice when your conversation is heading for a likely objection.

Remember, you're not responding to an objection; you're anticipating it. But even when your prospect objects before you can deliver your GPOS, you're ready to answer intelligently and positively.

Planning Guide: Genuine Preemptive Objection Statements (GPOS)

Make a list of some of the objections that commonly occur during your presentations, which you could use to give your customers key information. Write a GPOS for each objection.

What Did The Buyers Say?

from Marketshare Research Institute

The buyers we surveyed said that anticipating their objections in a positive way rated **6.89 out of 10**.

They said that **only 24% of reps** seemed to anticipate their objections this way.

(Averages of responses)

The Buyers Comment: GPOS

"Once a customer raises an issue, it becomes an objection. By bringing it up first, the sales rep keeps the customer from seeing it as a negative obstacle."

– Wm. Frank Quiett, C.P.M., A.P.P.
Project Lead, Supply Chain Management and Strategic Sourcing

"I think this a very good idea, as long as it is done sincerely and doesn't bash the competition. Many reps are well prepared to handle objections, but I've never experienced a rep presenting this in advance. It would save a lot of time."

– Henry Valiulus
Director of Purchasing

Create some effective questions for your prospect meetings

Secret 20

Properly-designed questions are one of your most effective meeting tools. As you create your questions, experiment with both closed-ended and open-ended questions.

Close-ended questions are usually answered with a simple one word answer—usually "yes" or "no":

- "Have you considered . . . ?"
- "Do you have plans to . . . ?"

These types of questions are useful for uncovering facts. However, be careful not to use too many of them in a row, or you'll sound like you're interrogating your prospect.

Open-ended questions—those that elicit an extended response—are more likely to tell you how your prospect thinks and what their needs are:

- "What do you like most about your [current process, website, etc.]?"
- "How would you describe your . . . ?"

Open-ended questions have many benefits:

- They encourage your prospect to become involved in the meeting rather than just being an audience.
- They stimulate your prospect to think about ways you can benefit them.
- They show you how your prospect perceives aspects of their business.

When you ask open-ended questions, it's important to let the prospect speak their mind without interrupting. Remember: It's just as important to let your prospects provide you information as it is for you to give it to them. Give them chances to speak, and listen. Only this way can you learn what your prospects really need and whether your products or services are a good fit for them.

Quality questions enhance your prospect's trust and your credibility. The more your prospect knows that *you* know about their specific needs, the more confident they are about your ability to solve their particular challenges.

Effective questioning allows the prospect to do most of the talking, and that is a recipe for success in a sales meeting. Bores talk about themselves; brilliant conversationalists focus on, and listen, to you.

When you do the talking, do you know for sure that people are actively listening? Asking questions guarantees your prospect's attention and participation.

In an initial meeting with a prospect, you must find answers to some specific questions. A good way to organize these questions is to use the time-honored formula journalists use to be sure they don't miss important information for their stories. This method uses the words what, who, when, where, why, and how.

Examples: Effective questions for prospect meetings

1. What is your prospect doing, or going to do, as it relates to your products and services?

2. With whom is your prospect working, or have they worked with in the past—and are they looking for someone now?

3. When is their buying cycle?

4. Where have they used a product or service similar to yours?

5. Why do they need your type of product or service?

6. How could your product or service be better-suited for the prospect's needs than what they currently use—and if it is, how does the prospect company make their buying decisions?

Once you've determined a potential fit, you can ask questions to see if there's an opportunity for you to do business with the prospect:

- "What is your definition of good [service/quality/etc.] ?"
- "What would it take for you to feel confident that we could handle your [type of product/service] needs?"
- "On what terms would you consider having us provide part of your [products/services] ?"
- "When it comes to selecting a supplier in this area, what are the most important factors in your decision?"

Be sure not to ask rhetorical questions (questions you intend to answer yourself), or manipulative questions. On the next page, you'll see some examples of good questions, provided by the buyers we interviewed for our book *Buyer-Approved Selling*.

What Did The Buyers Say?

from Marketshare Research Institute

The buyers we surveyed said that **only 42% of reps** asked good questions during meetings.

(Average of responses)

Examples from the Buyers:
Questions for prospect meetings

"What's the most important thing a supplier like us could do to help you and your company be more effective and profitable?"

— Trent N. Baker, C.P.M.
Purchasing Manager, Wilson Foods
Division of Reser's Fine Foods, Inc.

"What do I need to do to help you compare your present vendor's offering versus mine?"

— Scott Bartel
Sourcing Strategist

"I want to exceed your expectations: How would you go about defining a good supplier?"

— Lori Aljets
Purchasing and Quality Assurance Manager
Norpac Foods Inc.

"What do you look for when selecting a product or service?"

— Grahame Gill
Facilities Buyer

Be ready for tough questions from your prospects

Secret 21

Many business professionals have great verbal agility–but the best ones take the time to be sure their answers are the best they can be. There's nothing worse than being surprised by a tough question and having to struggle for an answer.

Examples: Tough questions

Here are some of the kinds of tough questions you may hear in a first meeting with a prospect:

- "I like your [product/service], but the VP at our head office makes these decisions. How do you think I can sell him on it?"
- "How can I be sure that you'll honor your [time guarantee, price guarantee, warranty etc.] ?
- "What if we experience crucial downtime with your [product/service] ? How quickly can you get us up and running again? Can you give me an example of how you've handled this with other clients?"
- "Can you prove to us that your company is financially stable enough to honor the [terms/warranty/agreement] for the full term of the contract?"

Assume responsibility for clear communication by making sure you've properly answered complex questions. In the natural flow of conversation, it's easy to jump from one issue to the next without any guarantee that both parties are "on the same page." Instead, confirm that your prospect understands by asking:

"Did I explain that clearly enough?"

Do *not* ask, "Did you get that okay?" (This can sound patronizing.)

What Did The Buyers Say?

from Marketshare Research Institute

The buyers we surveyed said that **32% of reps** had trouble answering questions they should have prepared for.

(Average of responses)

Examples from the Buyers: Tough Questions

Here are some more examples of tough prospect questions, courtesy of the buyers we interviewed for *Buyer-Approved Selling*.

"What differentiates your product from your competitor's?" (Chris adds: "I ask this of everyone in the first meeting.")

– CHRIS NIELD
CORPORATE BUYER, INTERNATIONAL TRUCK AND ENGINE CORP.

"How can your company increase my effectiveness, reduce costs, or improve customer satisfaction?"

– WM. FRANK QUIETT, C.P.M., A.P.P.
PROJECT LEAD, SUPPLY CHAIN MANAGEMENT AND STRATEGIC SOURCING

"How can you help me save money?"

– GRAHAME GILL
FACILITIES BUYER

"What is the value in your product/ service?"

— Jeff Hardman
Director of Network Operations

"Based on what you know about our firm, tell me why you think your product or service is right for us." (Mike adds: "The answer to this question tells me a lot—how much the seller has looked at our business situation, and whether their offering meets a real need, or is simply a 'hammer looking for a nail'.")

— Mike Kanze, C.P.M., A.P.P., MBA
President & CEO, Cornerstone Services Inc.

"What differentiates your product from similar products?" (Dean adds: "This moves the conversation toward value-added services like support staff, service department, and price. This question is very good, especially if the same equipment is supplied by different companies under different names.")

— Dean R. Schlosser, Jr.
Purchasing Agent

"Why do you think we will be successful if we choose your product?"
"Whom do you consider your competition?"

—Natalie Levy
V.P. Divisional Merchandise Manager, Lord and Taylor

"What exactly will you do in terms of support and follow-through?"

— Steve Mataya
Materials Manager, Allied Gear & Machine Co. Inc.

Planning Guide: Answers for tough questions

Make a list of some of the other tough questions you think your prospect could ask—and your answers to them.

"This is a ten out of ten. Most sales reps spend 15 minutes of my time going over brochures and talking about their company whether I know about them or not. I really like the idea of a single-page synopsis of company information."

– ANNE STILWELL, DIRECTOR
CONTRACT AND PROCUREMENT SERVICES, FANNIE MAE

Secret 22

Create a Company Information Sheet (CIS)

During sales presentations, buyers are often given pages and pages of information they don't have time to read. Our research shows that on initial sales calls, "less is more." A well-written Company Information Sheet helps you keep down the paperwork while being sure your prospect has essential information about your company.

Planning Guide: Company Information Sheet

Create your Company Information Sheet. List the following items on a single page, using bullet points:

- Your ISPS *(see page 26)* or your PRS *(see page 30)*
- The number of years your company has been in business
- An example of how your company gave ROI to a client in the prospect's industry
- A partial list of current clients—ideally, in the prospect's industry *(see page 72)*
- Any relevant company certifications or awards

The Buyers Comment: CIS

"Most reps send pages and pages of information about their company, and I don't have time for that. If they're trying to introduce their company, they should have the one-page summary. They should all be using this approach, but I've never met one who did."

– GENE ROBERTS
MANAGER OF PURCHASING

"It's a good idea. Short bullet-points and a single page are more likely to be read than pages of data about your company."

– LESLIE CHAMPION
SENIOR PROCUREMENT SPECIALIST
INDUSTRIAL DESIGN & CONSTRUCTION, INC.

"I first saw one last week. It's useful for comments and feedback as well. Only a small percentage of reps use this type of sales tool, and I'd like to see more of them. I'd give this a nine out of ten."

– ROY SEKIGAWA
PURCHASING OPERATIONS MANAGER
FOREMOST DAIRIES, HAWAII

"**Unfortunately, only about 10%** of my suppliers follow this procedure. If I could receive a schedule prior to the meeting and remove any content that would not be advantageous to me, it would certainly help the supplier, who could then spend more time on issues of interest to me."

– CHRISTOPHER LOCKE, GLOBAL LEAD BUYER
DAIMLERCHRYSLER CORPORATION

Use an Advance Meeting Agenda (AMA)

Meetings are part of business life, but many of them consume unnecessary time because they lack structure. Prior to each meeting, email your prospect an Advance Meeting Agenda and invite their changes.

Secret 23

An agenda should chronologically list your meeting's key topics. When you email your prospect an Advance Meeting Agenda, you:

- Show respect for the prospect's time and your interest in addressing the company's needs.
- Let the prospect feel more involved in the meeting process.
- Let the prospect prepare any required information.
- Show you have researched the company.
- Show that you are proactive, organized, and competent.

On the next page, you'll see an example of an email message with an AMA.

Example: Advance Meeting Agenda

```
┌─────────────────────────────────────────────────────────────────┐
│  ✎  Dec. 14 Meeting Agenda                              _ □ ☒   │
├─────────────────────────────────────────────────────────────────┤
│  File   Edit   Options   Window   Help                          │
├─────────────────────────────────────────────────────────────────┤
│  [toolbar icons]                                                 │
├─────────────────────────────────────────────────────────────────┤
│  From:     Cassandra Owens     ▼   Follow-up:    ▼              │
│  To:       Monica Smyth <msmyth@buyerco.com>                    │
│  Copy:                                   Blind Copy:            │
│  Subject:  Dec. 14 Meeting Agenda                               │
├─────────────────────────────────────────────────────────────────┤
```

Hello Monica,

I'm looking forward to meeting with you and Bryan. Your time is valuable, so I've prepared a basic agenda for our meeting. Please feel free to add items so we can address your needs more efficiently.

Meeting appointment:
  Date: Tuesday, Dec. 14, 2004
  Time/duration: 2:00-2:30 P.M.
  Place: 555 Vista Avenue, Suite 4000

Attendees:
  Monica Smyth, Marketing Manager, BuyerCo
  Bryan Bard, Marketing Coordinator, BuyerCo
  Cassandra Owens, President, SmallBizCo

Meeting objective:
  To determine if SmallBizCo is a good fit to provide BuyerCo's corporate travel services.

Order of business:
  1. Give a brief overview of SmallBizCo.
  2. Explore BuyerCo's corporate travel needs.
  3. Examine potential strategies to meet BuyerCo's travel requirements more efficiently and at lower cost.
  4. If it appears that SmallBizCo's services can be of specific value to BuyerCo, summarize those service details in a written proposal.

Warmly,
Cassandra Owens,
Corporate Account Executive, SmallBizCo
555-231-1234

```
├─────────────────────────────────────────────────────────────────┤
│  Signature:            ▼   □ View signature   ☑ Keep Copy    □ Return Rcpt.   □ Send Later: │
│                            □ Send vCard       □ Blind Send   □ Opened Rcpt.                  │
│                                                              NUM                             │
└─────────────────────────────────────────────────────────────────┘
```

What Did The Buyers Say?

from Marketshare Research Institute

The buyers we surveyed said that receiving meeting agendas
in advance rated **8.13 out of 10** in helpfulness.

(Average of responses)

The Buyers Comment: AMA

"It is easier to set up the attendee list when you have an agenda. It also allows adding to the agenda or removing what you don't want. At my company, no one has time to spend on meetings that do not specifically address their needs."

– Toni Horn, C.P.M.
Global Commodity Manager
Silicon Graphics Inc.

"I think it's great to know what the topics will be before the meeting. It shows that the sales rep is serious and prepared for the meeting."

– Natalie Levy
V.P. Divisional Merchandise Manager
Lord and Taylor

"Presented sufficiently in advance, it gives the buyer the opportunity to reject inappropriate agenda points or change them accordingly. It also forces the vendor to think rationally in advance about the meeting and to set realistic goals about the meeting's outcome."

– Mike Kanze, C.P.M., A.P.P., MBA
President & CEO, Cornerstone Services Inc.

"This is pretty important—it helps to keep you on track in the meeting, and it makes things much more efficient."

– Jim Morey
Vice President of Procurement
Sara Lee Foods, a division of Sara Lee Corporation

"It makes sense for businesspeople to start off with a brief introduction of their company. I can't tell them what my needs are until I know what they can offer."

– BRIAN MORAN, DIRECTOR AMERICAS SUPPLY MANAGEMENT
SIEMENS WESTINGHOUSE POWER CORPORATION

Prepare an overview of your company

Secret 24

When you map out your sales-meeting strategy, it's important to pay close attention to respect and courtesy. If you were a buyer meeting with a sales rep for the first time, how would you feel if the rep jumped right in and started "grilling" you about your company?

Before you start asking your prospect questions, be sure to earn the right to do so by establishing your credibility. You can do this by offering the buyer a brief overview of your company. This shows the buyer the benefits of answering your questions, and helps them feel more comfortable about continuing the conversation.

Example: Company overview

Here's a good way to present this initial overview:

"Mr. Prospect, before we get into the meeting, I was hoping I could share a few key points about [my company]. Would that be okay?"

[The prospect agrees]

"We specialize in saving accounting firms time and money on their travel arrangements. We've worked with XYZ Accounting Co and CBD Co, two of the largest accounting firms in the city. In fact, XYZ Accounting Co chose us out of five vendors, and we've been saving them 8% a month on their travel costs ever since. May I leave this company information sheet with you? Thanks. Now may I ask you a few questions about [your company]?"

Use this Planning Guide to prepare your own company overview.

Planning Guide: Company overview

Step 1: Write down ISPS *(see page 26)* or your PRS *(see page 30)*.

Step 2: Write the names of a few of your key accounts.

Step 3: Using the example from your Company Information Sheet, write a brief description of how your company provided ROI to a client in the prospect's industry.

Secret 25

Leave your prospect with some crucial questions for other vendors

Imagine you're a buyer. You've just had an initial meeting with a new rep. The rep left you with some objective questions that you could ask all potential vendors—some of which you had not considered, but which were intrinsic to a sound buying decision. Does that increase your confidence in the rep's ability to serve your needs?

Our research shows that buyers appreciate it when reps leave them with objective questions for vendors; they consider it "extra value" before the sale. By providing some important questions the buyer might not have considered, you can help them make a more informed decision.

At the end of the sales meeting, you can introduce your list of questions this way:

"Monica, I've put together a few questions that might be helpful in making your decision. They're objective questions that you should ask any vendor before you decide to move forward. May I leave them with you?"

Examples: Questions for Vendors

- "Can we view our account details online?"
- "What happens if you can't run our advertisements in the promised time slots?"
- "How do you measure the results of the training, and what kind of retention do you guarantee?"
- "What happens if you can't honor your service response-time guarantee?"
- "What happens if replacement parts are discontinued?"

- "What contingency plan do you have for downtime?"

- "Do you have tracking reports I can access online?"

- "What happens if we have an equipment failure? Does your company provide a loaner? If so, does it cost anything?"

- "When you service our equipment, do you use new or refurbished parts?"

- "Do you actively recycle your discarded parts? Do you have other environmental policies?"

Planning Guide: Objective questions for buyers

Create your own list of objective questions crucial to your buyers' decisions.

What Did The Buyers Say?

from Marketshare Research Institute

The buyers we surveyed gave a **rating of 6.33 out of 10** to the idea of reps leaving them with objective questions for vendors.

They said that **only 22% of reps** actually left them with objective questions.

(Averages of responses)

The Buyers Comment: Objective questions for vendors

"This could be very helpful, but be careful not to put down competitors in an effort to make your company look better. The right questions should be indicators that the seller has confidence that his or her company has the preferred response."

— KRISTEN MITCHELL
SENIOR BUYER
BOSTON FINANCIAL DATA SERVICES INCORPORATED

"Maybe they will bring up something we haven't considered. That would be helpful for us."

— RICHARD LUSK
DIRECTOR OF PURCHASING
LENNAR HOMES, INC.

"This would be valuable because different reps bring different experiences and perspectives to the table. Situations may have occurred elsewhere that have not (yet) occurred in the buyer's organization."

— EDWARD DiLELLO, C.P.M.
PROCUREMENT SPECIALIST
PHILADELPHIA GAS WORKS

"A testimonial letter on its own rates a 2 out of 10. The value of references we can call is a ten out of ten."

– JIM MOREY, VICE PRESIDENT–PROCUREMENT
SARA LEE FOODS, A DIVISION OF SARA LEE CORPORATION

Provide references your prospects can contact

Secret 26

It's a common belief that glowing testimonial letters can help influence a sale. But think about it: Have you ever read a bad testimonial? How useful are they as a sales tool?

When we interviewed our buyers, we found that they valued testimonial letters much less than they did appropriate references with whom they could speak directly. In general:

- Many buyers felt that testimonial letters had little or no impact on their decisions.

- Most buyers felt that appropriate, live references had significant influence on their decisions.

Imagine this scenario:

You're in an initial sales meeting. You've determined there is a fit, and the prospect has asked you to prepare a proposal.

As you're summarizing the requirements for the proposal, you offer the prospect the opportunity to call three of the clients on your Company Information Sheet. You invite them to select any three clients, and tell them you will include the contact information for these references in your proposal.

For each client on your reference page, include:

- The references' contact information
- Their products/services
- The number of years they have been your client
- A brief description of how your reference benefited from doing business with you.

Example: Client Reference Page

Client: XYZ Co., Mark Smith, V.P. of Procurement. (888) 888-8888.

Industry: Call Centers

Years as client: 3

Service provided: Long-Distance

Benefit to client: We saved XYZ Co. $10,000 over the last 3 years, with no downtime.

The Buyers Comment: Testimonials vs. references

"Testimonial letters or awards from other customers alone do not impress me. The above approach would be very effective in gaining my business."

– TONI HORN, C.P.M.
GLOBAL COMMODITY MANAGER
SILICON GRAPHICS INC.

"I much prefer talking to references and asking them questions directly. They need to be references that have something in common with my company or industry."

– JUDY ELRITE, C.P.M.
BUYER SPECIALIST

"I require the option of being able to telephone past clients–which I do follow up on. There are always production-related questions I need to ask that are not covered in the letters and testimonials."

– MICHAEL TATOR
V.P., DIRECTOR OF PRODUCTION
WUNDERMAN, OF THE Y&R COMPANIES, IRVINE

Create your meeting planner

We've covered a lot of ground preparing for an effective meeting. To help the meeting go as smoothly as possible, it's a good idea to prepare a meeting planner.

Secret 27

The planner is simply a binder or folder that organizes the items you need for a successful meeting. It contains a checklist and appropriate supporting documents, all of which we've discussed.

Use the Planning Guide on the next page to assemble your own meeting planner. Each item shows the page where it is described, and a document checklist is included.

What Did The Buyers Say?

from Marketshare Research Institute

The buyers we surveyed said that **40% of reps** were **clearly unprepared** for sales calls.

(Average of responses)

Planning Guide: Meeting planner (sample checklist)

- Advance Meeting agenda *(pg. 63)*
- Company overview *(pg. 67)*
- Company information sheet *(pg. 61)*
- Questions *(pg. 54)*
- Proposal required? Yes _____ No _____
- References *(pg. 72)*
- Summary of key points and action items *(pg. 77)*
- (Post-meeting) Send email summary *(pg. 80)*
- (Post-meeting) Prepare proposal *(pg. 84)*

Document checklist

- Copy of email agenda *(pg. 63)*
- Company information sheet *(pg. 61)*
- Question sheet *(pg. 54)*
- Answers to potential questions *(pg. 58)*
- Company research sheet *(pg. 47)*
- Crucial Questions sheet *(pg. 69)*

"**When you conclude a meeting,** it makes sense to confirm the key points discussed. It's important that all parties are confident that real communication has taken place. A concise summary is an ideal way to achieve this goal."

– ANDREW JULES DEGIULIO, PURCHASING MANAGER

End your meeting with a verbal key-point summary

Secret 28

So far, so good. You took the time to plan and prepare for your meeting. Now it's time to wrap it up and honor the time commitment in your meeting agenda.

To put the perfect finish on a job well-done, you need to take care of one last detail: Summarize the key points you discussed to ensure that both you and your prospect understand them.

Example: Key-point summary

Here's an example of how you could present a key-point summary at the end of a meeting.

"John, just to be sure I haven't missed anything, I'd like to recap the key points of our meeting:

"Tomorrow morning, I'm going to call Tracy Jackson to find out how much of your monthly long distance is affected by the current 1-minute minimum; then I'll put together a written comparison which will compare what you're currently paying with our 3-second minimum billing format. I'll have the comparison in your Inbox by 3 P.M. tomorrow.

"Then on Thursday I will meet with Kevin Lee, your operations manager, at your branch office in Richmond and conduct the same review I did with Tracy.

"And by Friday, at 3 P.M., I'll have a proposal at your office, which will include the required hardware costs.

"Does that cover everything, or is there anything I might have missed?"

Note: When appropriate, summarize key points at the end of a telephone meeting as well.

What Did The Buyers Say?

from Marketshare Research Institute

The buyers we surveyed said that a verbal summary of a meeting's key points rated **8.42 out of 10** in helpfulness.

They said that **only 42% of reps** gave them verbal summaries of their meetings.

(Averages of responses)

The Buyers Comment: End-of-meeting summaries

"Summarizing at the end of a meeting has great value. If I were to do sales training, this is one of the top skills I would definitely teach. It keeps both sides on track and becomes a very effective tool when confirmed via email. I use it today as an action-item checklist."

— Lynne E. Gehrke
Vice President, Procurement
A. B. Dick Company

"Only about 5-10% of the people I meet with actually make sure that we've communicated clearly on all points. It's important to summarize what was discussed and identify the next steps."

— Kenneth F. Esbin
Purchasing Manager
Tarmac America

"Summarizing key points gives me a chance to confirm expectations from the meeting and allows me to respond with any additions or changes I might have."

— Peggy Jones
Operations/H.R. Director
Magic Software Enterprises, Inc.

"An email summary would be very helpful; it's always good to have written clarification of key points. It shows they're paying attention and that they're on top of things. In five years, perhaps 2% of the reps I've met with have ever emailed a written summary of key points after a meeting."

– KRISTEN MITCHELL, SENIOR BUYER
BOSTON FINANCIAL DATA SERVICES INC.

Email your prospect a follow-up summary

Secret 29

You're heading back to the office after a great meeting. Your next step is to email your prospect the key points you summarized at the end of the meeting. By doing so, you:

- Show your proactivity and attention to detail.
- Ensure effective communication and accountability.
- Give your prospect a chance to add any additional points.

On the next page, you'll see an example of such an email message.

Example: Follow-Up Summary

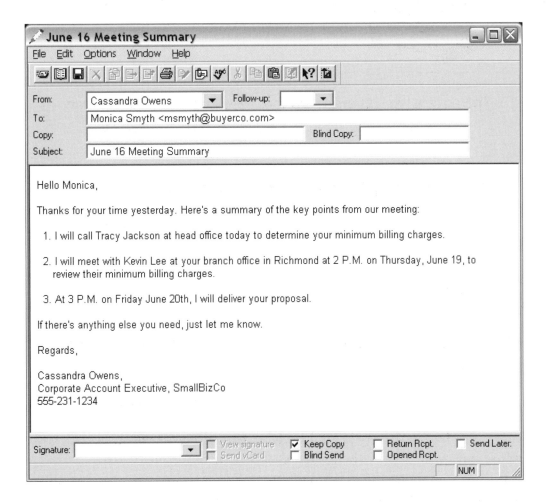

What Did The Buyers Say?

from Marketshare Research Institute

The buyers we surveyed said that receiving an email summary after a meeting rated **8.13 out of 10** in helpfulness.

They said that **only 24% of reps** sent summaries after meetings.

(Averages of responses)

The Buyers Comment: Email summaries

"I find this very useful, since it allows me to start an email file to keep track of my relationship with the vendor."

– Ken Fuqua
Purchasing Administrator

"That would be great—very helpful, because many times we put stuff aside when we are busy with all the things going on in our department. There is always something that we need to focus our attention on, so when we get the email it's just nice to have that to refer back to when necessary."

– Krysia Diaz, CEBS
Benefits Supervisor

"I always ask for a follow-up email from the rep after the meeting to help me communicate with my colleagues and keep everything organized and filed."

– RANDY SHEPHERD
SYSTEMS COORDINATOR, SENIOR BUYER

"**The proposal is important** when determining which vendors should be short-listed. When certain buying decisions are shared, a properly detailed proposal is valuable because it addresses the concerns of all the departments involved."

— DEAN R. SCHLOSSER, JR., PURCHASING AGENT

For more sales, consider a strategic proposal

Secret 30

Your planning and preparation paid off with a well-orchestrated meeting. You asked the right questions, said the right things, and confirmed an opportunity to help the buyer increase revenues or decrease costs. Your prospect has requested a proposal—you're on the short list.

When it comes to creating proposals, many companies use preset formats that suit most selling situations. For more complex sales, however, consider a strategic proposal.

Keep in mind that strategic proposals are not necessary for all sales. Use shorter proposals when appropriate—but be sure to present them on your letterhead, not on the back of a brochure or on a fax cover page (as I have seen many times!). A nice touch is to add your prospect's logo to the cover page or body of your proposal by cutting and pasting it from their website.

We are fortunate to present some fine information about strategic proposals from Robert F. Kantin, a recognized expert in sales proposals. Bob is president of SalesProposals.com and the author of several sales-proposal books, including *Sales Proposals Kit for Dummies.*

From *Strategic Proposals: Closing the Big Deal* by Robert F. Kantin

Sales professionals may do everything right during the sale, but if they don't integrate the development of a strong, strategic proposal into the process, they put their sales at risk.

Strategic Proposal Structure

A strategic proposal contains five main sections. These sections are interrelated and customer-focused. They categorize information and provide a logical sequence of information and ideas.

1. **Background Information** identifies the buyer's current situation, the improvement opportunity—the buyer's unresolved problem or unachieved opportunity, and the basis for the proposal. Some recommended Section 1 subsections include:

   - Industry Background
   - Client/Customer Background
   - Current Operations or Functions
   - Improvement Opportunity [Definition, Analysis, and Plans]
   - Client/Customer Needs and Objectives
   - Purpose of This Proposal

2. **Proposed Business Solution** presents the seller's proposed custom application of their products or services, and details how the seller will help the buyer achieve the improvement opportunity.

   Section 2 of a strategic proposal should contain four recommended subsections:

   - Product or Service Description
   - Product of Service Application

- Non-financial (Qualitative) Benefits
- Financial (Quantitative) Benefits

3. **Implementation Management** presents the seller's implementation methodology or project management practices and schedules to assure the buyer that the seller is able to deliver on the contract.

Like the first two strategic proposal sections that have definite subsection requirements, the third proposal section has three recommended subsections:

- **Methods:** implementation, project, engagement, or management methods (or practices)
- **Team:** implementation, project, engagement, or client service team
- **Schedule:** implementation, project, or engagement schedule

4. **Seller Profile** discusses the seller's qualifications and business practices to further assure the buyer that the seller will be able to deliver on the contract and provide ongoing service.

This section has six suggested subsections:

- Mission or Customer Service Philosophy Statement
- Company or Corporate Overview
- Quality
- Customer References
- Why us?
- Design and Development Checklist

5. **Business Issues** profiles the seller's business and groups all business-related items for ease of review and reference, such as fees/prices, as-

sumptions used for scheduling and pricing expenses, and when and how the seller will invoice the buyer.

Most sellers will find that three subsections suffice in the last strategic proposal section:

- Assumptions: i.e. to adhere to the implementation schedule, a software development consultant might assume the buyer will review and approve design documents within five business days of receipt.
- Fees/Prices and Other Expenses
- Invoicing Schedule

Proposal Components

Additionally, a strategic proposal should include the following components:

- **Title Page**
- **Executive Summary**—as its name implies, a concise synopsis of the entire proposal
- **Table of Contents**—a listing of main sections and subsections with page numbers
- **Appendices**—used to support information contained in the main proposal sections; a place for preprinted form, detailed financial calculations, product specifications, etc.

Use Appendices for Preprinted Materials

The overall appearance of a proposal is ruined when the seller includes preprinted materials in main proposal sections. Preprinted materials will interrupt a proposal's flow of information and ideas. Often when a writer puts a brochure or specifications sheet in the middle of a proposal section, he or she wants the recipient to find crucial information in the document. The recipient would be better served if the seller summarized the information in one or two paragraphs and used the preprinted material as a supporting appendix.

Proposal Structure at a Glance

I. Executive Summary

II. Background Information

    a. Industry Information

    b. Background

    c. Current Operation or Functions

    d. Improvement Opportunity [definition, analysis, and plans]

    e. Needs and Objectives [buyer]

    f. Purpose of this Proposal

III. Proposed Solution

    a. Product or Service Description

    b. Product or Service Application (optional)

    c. Nonfinancial Benefits

    d. Financial Benefits

IV. Implementation

    a. Engagement or Project Management Methods

    b. Schedule

    c. Team

V. Seller Profile

    a. Mission Statement

    b. Company Profile

    c. Quality

    d. Why Us?

    e. Other subsections based on the seller's industry or profession

VI. Business Issues

    a. Assumptions

    b. Fees/Prices [and other expenses]

    c. Invoicing Schedule

VII. Appendices

Our thanks to Bob Kantin for allowing us to include this important material. You can reach him at:

13646 East Laurel Lane
Scottsdale, AZ 85259
480-636-1210 • www.salesproposals.com

What Did The Buyers Say?
from Marketshare Research Institute

The buyers we surveyed said that the quality of sales proposals rated **7.53 out of 10** in influencing their buying decisions.

They said that **only 54% of reps** provided them with quality proposals.

(Averages of responses)

The Buyers Comment: Proposal quality

"Proposals are very important as they help us create a short list of the top two or three vendors. These vendors get the opportunity to come in and do a formal presentation."

– KRISTEN MITCHELL
SENIOR BUYER
BOSTON FINANCIAL DATA SERVICES INCORPORATED

"The proposal is very important—a nine or ten out of ten. The proposal provides an opportunity for potential suppliers to do their homework, demonstrate their knowledge, and clearly articulate their value proposition to our buying group. "

– GREG TENNYSON, C.P.M., CPCM
VICE PRESIDENT, CORPORATE PROCUREMENT
ORACLE CORPORATION

"A good proposal tells me a great deal about the company's professionalism. If they have a professional presentation, it tells me they care about their company's perception in the marketplace. "

– KENNETH F. ESBIN
PURCHASING MANAGER
TARMAC AMERICA

Secret 31

Closing: Keep it simple

Closing the sale—there are entire books and seminars dedicated to it. You may have heard of some of these unusual-sounding techniques:

- The Red Herring Close
- The Secondary Question Close
- The Sharp Angle Close
- The Lost Sale Close
- The Affirmative No Close
- The Similar Situation Close
- The Buying Criteria Close
- The Assumptive Close
- The Ben Franklin Close
- The Value Added Close
- The Instant Reverse Close
- The Change Places Close

But closing is more about the journey than the destination. If you've presented your information well, communicated clearly, and determined that a sale is in the buyer's best interests, closing should be simple and straightforward. For example:

"I'd like to go ahead and book this order. Does that work for you?"

In the course of our research, we submitted these closing questions to our buyers and asked for their comments:

A. We can start the project on the 15th, no problem. Is there anything else you need to know to move ahead?

B. If we can start the project on the 15th, can you think of any reason why we shouldn't set it up now?

C. Let's start the project on the 15th—is that okay?

What Did The Buyers Say?

from Marketshare Research Institute

71% of the buyers preferred **closing question A.**

Question A was provided by Art Sobczak, president of Business by Phone Inc. Our thanks to him for allowing us to include this valuable material. You can reach Art at:

Business By Phone Inc.
13254 Stevens St.
Omaha, NE 68137

402-895-9399

www.businessbyphone.com

The Buyers Comment: Closing the sale

"Question A rates 10 out of 10. It illustrates that you can provide the service on the terms the buyer needs, and the open-ended question allows communication. It's informal, flows well, and it's not pushy."

– KATHI WILSON
FACILITIES ASSISTANT
IDX SYSTEMS CORPORATION

"Question A is 9 out of 10. It sounds more professional, more customer service-oriented. Question B, 'Can you think of any reason why we shouldn't set it up now?', sounds a little pushy."

– LISA PERDUE
SENIOR BUYER

"I give Question A 10 out of 10. It's more subtle than the other two questions. I like the way it asks the buyer if there is anything more that the selling company can do."

– PHYLLIS PIERCE
PURCHASING/ACCOUNTS RECEIVABLE MANAGER

"With most companies, there is not enough follow-up after the sale. Service after the sale is just as important as service before the sale. Buyers want to know that the people they are dealing with, and investing their money and time in, are going to be around for the long term."

— TRENT N. BAKER, C.P.M., PURCHASING MANAGER
WILSON FOODS, DIVISION OF RESER'S FINE FOODS, INC.

Keep your customers happy

You're probably aware that it takes less time and money to keep an existing customer than to create a new one. Now that you've gone to so much trouble to create new customers, be sure you don't "orphan" them.

Secret 32

It's tremendously important to stay in tune with your customers' needs. Besides the obvious benefits of additional revenue, happy customers often provide quality referrals, leading to the rapid broadening of your business as one referral yields another.

Buyers and other decision-makers do their colleagues a valuable favor by referring exceptional suppliers. When it works out, it makes them look good and everyone benefits.

That's why it's very important to keep track of how your customers feel about you. "You don't need expensive surveys and complex statistical models," Fred Reichheld says in the Harvard Business Review (Dec. 2003). "You only have to ask your customers one question: 'How likely is it that you would recommend our company to a friend or a colleague?'"

You can do that with a simple phone call. If a customer gives you a very short answer, go deeper and ask what they actually like (or dislike) about your service.

Another way to track customer satisfaction is with a brief email message at appropriate intervals. This lets your customers know they are valued, and you may get the chance to nip any problems in the bud.

Example: "Checking in" email message

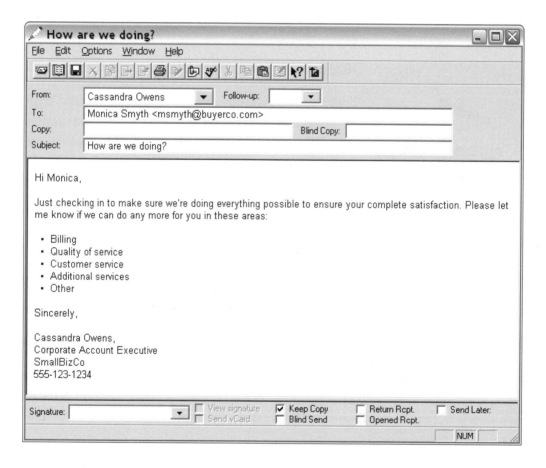

Another way to build strong business relationships and customer loyalty is to provide your customers with useful information and resources. For example:

- Forwarding your customers noteworthy articles or information relevant to their industry

- Sending them referrals

- Conducting brief information-based seminars—at your office, their office, or a large venue for hosting many customers at once—where you offer them true business value in your field of expertise.

- Provide a webpage with free, useful information. (For an excellent example see www.bizstats.com. Operated by Patrick O'Rourke CPA, and his company, cpa2go, it offers professional accounting services and free business and educational resources.)

 **What Did The Buyers Say?**

from Marketshare Research Institute

The buyers we surveyed said that post-sale follow-up rated **8.08 out of 10** in importance to them.

They said that **only 48% of reps** verified their satisfaction after sales and periodically contacted them to assure ongoing satisfaction.

(Averages of responses)

Tying It All Together

This section contains key secrets you can use to make Parts 1 and 2 even more effective.

Emerson said, "Common sense is as rare as genius." Like the other methods in this book, those that follow are based on common sense, and they're essential for creating a customer-approved business. Yet far too many businesspeople ignore them or simply aren't aware of them.

Remember, it's one thing to have information and another to use it. So please read, enjoy, and employ the following pages. They contain a wealth of beneficial, practical information that will serve you well in your journey to success.

"Follow-up is tremendously important and an email would be fine. I'll give you an example of what happens more often than not: I ask for a usage history or some other documentation, and they pass it on to their administrative staff. Then they walk in the next month and say, 'So what can we do for you?' I say, 'I'm still waiting for that usage report from last month,' and he says, 'What do you mean? I told my office to take care of that.' Why didn't he take ownership and follow up for me with his own company?"

– KENNETH F. ESBIN
PURCHASING MANAGER, TARMAC AMERICA

Commit to a target date and confirm completion

Dependability is a valued commodity–yet it's not uncommon for businesspeople to make promises they don't keep.

Secret 33

The problem is time. There's never enough—and so an unscheduled item on a to-do list routinely gets bumped by items that do have target dates. By committing to a target date for each of your promises, you:

- Learn to be more realistic
- Learn to better manage your time
- Become accountable!

Depending on the situation, the next step in your sales process can be to confirm completion of the promised task via email or with a short voice-mail message.

What Did The Buyers Say?

from Marketshare Research Institute

The buyers we surveyed said that when a sales rep called to confirm the fulfillment of a promise, it rated **8.9 out of 10.**

They said that **only 48% of reps** consistently called to confirm fulfillment of their promises.

(Averages of responses)

The Buyers Comment: Confirming promises

"I like this approach because it suggests they are competent professionals who follow through, and that raises my comfort level."

– GREG GRAHAM
BUYER, KENWORTH TRUCK COMPANY

"I like to hear from reps so that I can pass the information on to the appropriate people in my company who want to know the promised transaction has been completed. It helps keep me on top of things. I deal with several reps that don't always follow through on promises and I find that extremely annoying."

– ALAN B. RIFKIN
SENIOR BUYER

"Accountability is essential to the business transaction. It flows both ways, as does respect. A sales person who sets a realistic target date and confirms completion earns my respect, and therefore the privilege to expand the business relationship."

–ANDREW JULES DEGIULIO
PURCHASING MANAGER

Secret 34

Under-promise and over-deliver

In the heat of the moment, it's common for businesspeople to make promises they can't realistically keep—or at least not in the exact way they were given. A customer may not get mad about such a discrepancy; however, it's likely they'll make a mental note of it, and even mention it to others. Often all it takes are one or two broken promises for a customer to start saying "yes" to your competition.

If you're having trouble meeting the target dates you promise (as discussed in Secret 33), you may need to get into the habit of under-promising and over-delivering. That way, everybody wins. Your customers actually get better service or quality than they expect, and you keep their trust.

"**I don't return messages** that are not decipherable, use poor grammar, or make no real point. You have only one opportunity to get it right—so rehearse the call, and make sure that what you say has substance."

– Errol van Edema, Manager of Purchasing
& Manufacturing/Distribution

Rehearse your important voice-mail messages

Considering the importance of voice mail, there is a real lack of guidance in the art of leaving effective messages.

Secret 35

How often have you had to play a voice-mail message several times before you could understand the caller's name or phone number? How many rambling, unplanned messages have you had to endure?

It's important to avoid this pitfall with your own voice-mail messages. Here are some key steps to ensure clarity and professionalism:

1. **Plan and prepare.** Before you make the call, assume your prospect is busy and that you will have to leave a message. Write out your message's essential points.

2. **Rehearse, or role-play with a colleague.** A quick run-through helps ensure your message is clear and concise.

3. **Start and end the message with your contact info.** Including your name, company name, and phone number at the beginning *and* end of your message lets your prospect check the info for accuracy and makes it unnecessary for them to replay the message if they miss anything.

4. **When you leave your contact info, slow down.** Most people can't write as quickly as people speak. When you leave your contact info, imagine you're writing it down too. (Don't speak ridiculously slowly, though; that can be just as annoying, and even seem patronizing.)

What Did The Buyers Say?

from Marketshare Research Institute

The buyers we surveyed said that effective voice-mail messages rated **8.28 out of 10** in importance.

They said that **32%** of voice-mail messages from reps were hard to understand, lacked key information, or had to be played several times to hear a name or number.

(Averages of responses)

The Buyers Comment: Effective voice mail

"Many people do not rehearse what they are going to say, or they speak way too fast. Keep messages short and sweet, and leave a telephone number only if (1) it is a local telephone call; or (2) it is an 800 number. Don't ask customers to return your call long-distance."

– Beckie Beard, C.P.M, A.P.P., CACM
Director, Purchasing & Materials Management
Lansing Community College

"I think that messages should be clear and to-the-point. I receive many calls throughout the day, and I don't have time to listen to someone go on and on."

– Lou Riley
Senior Director, Materials Management

"Most reps say the phone number so fast that it takes three listens to get it. If the message is poorly delivered, I won't return the call. My job is phone-intensive and I'm very busy."

– Judy Elrite, C.P.M.
Buyer Specialist

Record your role-plays to improve your communication skills

Secret 36

When you record role-plays of typical business calls with the help of a friend or colleague, it can help you improve your ability to communicate effectively and intelligently.

When you listen to your own phone technique, you may discover communication habits you were unaware of and could improve. Most people who take the time to record themselves report dramatic improvements in their confidence and communication skills—and as a result, they make more appointments and close more sales. When you listen to your recordings, check for these signs:

- Are you speaking too quickly?
- Do you sound unsure of yourself?
- Do you speak in a monotone?
- Do you sound insincere?
- Do you interrupt the other person?
- Could you convey more energy and impact, where appropriate?

Identify and eliminate weak words and phrases

Referring to your taped role-plays *(see pg. 108)*, identify and work on eliminating weak, indecisive phrases and words such as these:

- "Do you know what I mean?"
- "To tell you the truth . . ."
- "To be honest . . ."
- "You know?"
- "I guess"
- "I hope"
- "I think"
- "Maybe"
- "Sort of"
- "Kind of"
- "Probably"
- "Possibly"
- "Basically"
- "Hopefully"

Planning Guide: Eliminating weak words and phrases

Write down some of the weak words and phrases that you tend to use and would like to remove from your business vocabulary. Simply identifying them can make you more aware of how often you use them.

Understand the 80/20 Principle—and live it

Secret 38

Do you feel like you consistently spend your time on activities that produce the best results for your business? At the end of a day, if you objectively examine how you spent your time, you may see that you have spent too much of it on things with low payoff.

As a business-owner, there are certain things you can handle best. It's vital that you identify the areas that bring you closer to your business objectives and focus your time there. It's way too easy to consume your time dealing with petty problems and other tasks that are best delegated to others or done after business hours. Be sure you weigh the true cost of misusing your valuable time, and consider that every hour you spend on low-return activities detracts from the high-return activities you should be focusing on.

The 80/20 Principle can help. Also referred to as Pareto's Principle, it was conceived by the Italian economist Vilfredo Pareto in 1906. Pareto observed that 20% of the population possessed 80% of the wealth. As a business-management tool, this principle suggests that:

- 20% of our activities create 80% of our results. That means that 80% of our activities create only 20% of our results.

- The 80/20 Principle can be applied to many areas of your business and personal life.

A number of books focus on this concept, if you wish to explore it more deeply. For our purposes, you just need to focus on the 20% of your activities that make a difference to your business objectives.

Secret 39

Prioritize your task list

No doubt about it: Time is the currency of life and business—and there never seems to be enough. It's vital to manage your time effectively. That means creating and using a prioritized task list every business day.

Here's a process you can use to organize each day's tasks and use your time as effectively as possible.

Step 1: With the 80/20 Principle in mind, take 5 to 10 minutes at the end of each day to make a complete list of the tasks you want to achieve the next day. Listing a day's tasks the night before offers these advantages:

- It's easier to remember unfinished tasks that need to be completed.
- It allows your subconscious mind to process ("sleep on") your list of items during the night.
- The next morning, you can add any items you might have missed.

Step 2: Plan an additional 5 to 10 minutes at the start of the next day to break your list into two groups:

Group A—Tasks that must absolutely be done that day

Group B—Everything else

Step 3: Prioritize Group A in order of importance. You should be able to find at least 6 items that are a "must do" each and every business day. Don't allow interruptions and time-wasters to get in the way of doing them.

Step 4: Now prioritize Group B, and begin them only if you've completed all items in Group A.

Can it be that simple? Absolutely—but only if you follow this process every day. No one can make you do it but you.

If I had eight hours to chop down a tree, I'd spend six sharpening my axe.

— ABRAHAM LINCOLN

As a team, plan the work and work the plan

Secret 40

It's not uncommon for people at work to feel they are in the business of being busy: answering the phone, answering email, dealing with interruptions . . . When the end of the day arrives and there is no clear record of achievement, you may ask yourself if your staff members were engaged in the work that truly mattered.

If that sounds familiar, it may be time to examine your company's (or department's) approach to work. As Michael Gerber so clearly says in his book *The E-Myth Revisited:* "You need to spend some time working *on* the business as opposed to always working *in* it."

Here's a two-step process we use at Approved Group Inc. to ensure we stay focused on achieving our company goals:

Step 1:

    a. Create a master list of all active projects.

    b. Create and title a master project document for each project.

    c. In each of these documents—beginning with the desired result and working your way backward—list all the things that must be done to achieve the project's goal. Identify the people responsible for each step.

Step 2:

    a. Each day, update the company's (or department's) master task list—preferably on a large whiteboard that everyone can see—with the appropriate tasks from your master project documents.

    b. For each task in the list, write the name of the person who will perform the task, a scheduled start time, and an estimated completion time.

    c. Prioritize each task as you did in your own task list *(see pg. 111)*.

    d. As tasks are completed through the day, check them off. This helps you keep track of progress and gives you a sense of achievement.

Summary

It's important to note that the 80/20 Rule *(see pg. 110)* applies here, too. Even if it takes up to 20% of your day to "sharpen the company axe" before you go into action, it can be time well-spent if it enables you to get the right results the first time. At our company, we have found this process extremely helpful.

Have fun and be authentic

Back in the introduction, I pointed out that this book had a theme that tied everything together:

Secret 41

For your business to be as successful as possible, you must be sure that your customers find your company easy and enjoyable to deal with.

Consider the flip side: If you're not having fun, pressure and stress are probably taking over, and those are definitely not ingredients for a Customer-Approved business.

It's virtually impossible to be a business-owner and not feel stressed, at least occasionally. It's a challenge, but it's absolutely vital that any stress you feel must not rub off during your interactions with your prospects, customers, suppliers, or employees. Similarly, you cannot permit your employees to become so stressed or dissatisfied that they transfer their tension to others. If either of these occur, it will damage your business. That's reality.

One of the keys to managing day-to-day stress at your business is the idea of having fun. While it's important not to go overboard and give your business too casual an image, it's also risky to approach prospects and customers in an overly-stilted manner.

The key is to stay genuinely focused on your business and your customers' needs while allowing your employees, and yourself, to relax and be who you are. Remember, businesses are made up of people, and people like the human connection that occurs when we are ourselves.

The message here is to remove the typical façade or "business mask" from your dealings with people. As the highly-successful business coach Christopher Flett says, "Be authentic." I can't stress this enough.

If you have any doubts about this approach, just call my friend and colleague Mitch Merker, VP and COO of Approved Publications. He takes business very seriously—yet he always has people smiling or laughing within a minute of speaking with him. People look forward to dealing with him because he makes it easier for them to be themselves, too.

Secret 42

Position yourself as an expert

People prefer to deal with experts. Experts often command a premium in the marketplace. So why not become one yourself by leveraging your experience and industry-specific knowledge?

Rather than trying to learn everything about everything, it's usually better to focus on a specific area of your industry or business with the goal of mastering it completely. If you can find an aspect of your field that particularly interests you—one with a demand for experts—you've found the best kind of area to focus on.

Example: Positioning yourself as an expert

You own a lawn-care company with a residential client base. You want to expand into the corporate market but you're having credibility challenges. You ask yourself, "What niche of my industry can I become an expert in to boost my company's credibility?"

You remember that some of your existing customers have asked you about composting, an area that interests you—so you decide to investigate the merits of becoming a composting expert. You do some research and learn that gardening magazines and newspaper gardening sections publish stories on composting, and that TV and radio gardening shows cover the subject too. You decide to study composting, knowing that there is an opportunity to learn what you need and to have outlets for publicizing your articles.

After extensive research and homework, you feel like you have earned the right to call yourself a composting expert, and you are ready to make your move. Here's a possible scenario:

- You write some articles on composting and eventually get them published.

- You market yourself to be interviewed on radio and or TV.

- You conduct mini-seminars at local gardening stores.

- You conduct seminars at gardening-related trade shows.

- You create a brochure that mentions all of these accomplishments, with specific details that can be validated.

- You follow the Customer-Approved sales approaches in this book and leverage your expertise as you call on corporate accounts.

- You win corporate accounts.

Taking this to the next level, you could write a book on your area of expertise and use it as an effective "business card."

Secret 43

Schedule your prospecting calls daily

If you're serious about developing new business, you must reach out and call prospects as discussed in Secret 13 *(pg. 33)*.

Most sales reps and businesspeople don't enjoy cold-calling. Many of them try to replace it with other, less-productive business development methods.

Many people are afraid of rejection, and take the word "no" too personally. But just wait until you make an appointment with a key account that brings revenue and prestige to your company. You may get a new attitude about cold calls!

In my 20-plus years in corporate sales—and now as a business-owner myself—I have made countless phone connections that have led to meetings, subsequent sales, and ongoing business relationships with Fortune 500 customers.

If you're willing to do it, calling works. Obviously, not everyone needs your products or services, but calling is your best way to connect with those who do.

It's hardly a secret, yet many people fail to act on this tremendously important principle: To be successful, you must do certain things that are outside of your comfort zone—and you can become comfortable with new activities only by making them routine.

As author David Joseph Schwartz (*The Magic of Thinking Big*) says, "To increase fear, wait, put off, postpone . . . To fight fear, act."

Commit yourself to a daily goal of a specific number of prospecting calls. Daily goals are more empowering than weekly or monthly goals. If your initial goal is just five calls per day, in one month you'll have 100 calls under your belt. Imagine what that could mean for your business development.

So start off with a calling goal that is relatively painless and achievable, and simply add one call per day until you are at your desired production level. Make it easy on yourself and you'll increase your chances of success.

Secret 44

Key decisions:
The two essential questions

The quality of your decisions can be the difference between success and failure. When you are faced with a key decision, ask yourself two questions:

1. What is the cost of doing it?

2. What is the cost of *not* doing it?

You may remember these two questions from Secret 2 *(pg. 8)*. They're extremely helpful in weighing the pros and cons of key decisions. Too often people look only at the cost of doing something, and not at the cost of not doing it.

When you use these questions to help you make business decisions, don't consider only the obvious factors like money. Be sure to include "soft" costs such as these:

- Time

- Effect on business relationships

- Lost opportunity

- Impact on corporate culture and morale

Secret 45

Appreciate and recognize your staff

The need for appreciation is one of the most fundamental human needs. To ignore it is to stifle enthusiasm and potential. Business is all about people, so look for opportunities to recognize your team members for jobs well-done.

Many people who like their jobs say they do so because they feel valued. Many of them say that feeling they make a difference at work, and being appreciated for their efforts and skills, *means more to them than money*.

It's been said that if you treat your employees like you treat your best customers, they'll treat your customers the same way. Makes sense to me!

If it's not part of your company culture to express appreciation to your employees, it would be wise to examine your work environment and make some adjustments. I can say this with conviction, from personal experience: Making your employees feel good about their work is "the difference that makes all the difference."

While appreciating and motivating people is not an exact science, here are a few ideas to consider:

- Recognize birthdays with a card signed by everyone.
- Reward the achievement of significant goals with a paid day off.
- Recognize achievements with a handwritten note from the owner or manager.
- Occasionally, reward achievement with flexible schedules.
- On a sunny day, take your team to the park for a one-hour brainstorming session about making the company more successful. (Your team will appreciate the chance to be heard.)

Secret 46

Keep your employees informed

Studies have shown that it is tremendously important to keep employees informed about events and developments in their company. Many employees feel that staying informed is a vital part of their working lives.

If you've ever worked at a company and heard something "through the grapevine" rather than from an official source, you know the negative feelings that such indirect communication can cause.

Unless it's confidential, it's important to promptly share any information that affects your employees or the business they work for. This creates trust, and contributes to the positive corporate culture that is the foundation of success.

Here are some suggestions for keeping your employees "in the know":

- Internal newsletter (print or email)
- Weekly or monthly "in the know" meetings where employees can ask any questions they want
- An "open door" policy where employees are encouraged to ask questions of management
- Bulletin boards with up-to-date information

If you want to know your past life, look into your present condition; if you want to know your future, look into your present action.

– Padmisambha

Have clear goals—in writing

Commitment, combined with clarity and focus, is a powerful force. Without written goals, you may find yourself off-course more often than not.

Secret 47

The vast majority of people do not have specific, measurable, achievable written goals. How many people do you know who do? Yet there is no doubt that people with written goals consistently outperform those who do not, by astounding margins.

In 1953, Yale's graduating seniors were interviewed to determine how many of them had clearly written goals. The answer was a dismal 3%. Twenty years later, researchers surveyed the surviving members of the Class of 1953 and discovered that the 3% with written goals had accumulated more wealth than the other 97% *combined*.

If you don't have a goal-setting system in place, here is one you can use. I used it when I decided to stop talking about writing a book, and to get on with the task of actually writing one.

It's funny, but when you get moving and take action, the first steps are always the hardest. This book you're reading is my fourth. Each one is less and less daunting—and I owe it all to the power of my written goals, which got me started and helped keep me going. (Of course I had immeasurable help from many people along the way—but nothing would have happened without the goals.)

The Written Goal System

Step 1: Record today's date; then below it, describe your goal in detail. What do you specifically want to achieve? Be sure it is *measurable* and *achievable*.

Step 2: List a forecasted completion date for your goal.

Step 3: List the amazing feelings and benefits of achieving your goal. Write these in strong emotional terms. For example: "I will feel supremely empowered, confident, and fulfilled by achieving my goal of . . ." Try to list 3 to 5 of these benefits.

Step 4: List the negative, miserable feelings and costs to your self-image of not carrying out the required actions (which you'll describe in the next step). Write these, too, in strong emotional terms. For example: "I will feel horrible if I don't honor my promise to myself. I will feel I am not living up to my potential—that I let myself and my company down by not following through on my commitment . . ." Try to list 3 to 5 negative consequences.

There is a very good reason for making this process as emotionally real for yourself as possible. Our decisions to tackle important new endeavors—as well as to avoid them—have strong emotional components. By systematically connecting with your desires in a positive way, and your fears in a negative way, you tap into the source of your motivation and use it to your advantage. Many people have immeasurably improved their lives this way—and so can you.

Keep in mind, too, that courage does not mean not being afraid. It means *acting in spite of your fears*. (The great American flying ace Eddie Rickenbacker said, "There can be no courage unless you're scared.") The key is to realize that, in the long run, failure to act is more painful—and that acting and succeeding makes everything else worthwhile.

Step 5: List all of the actions you must take to make your goal a reality. Be specific as possible. If this includes getting rid of your TV set, do it! (I did.)

In conclusion: You may not have control over all the outcomes of your goals. For example, if your goal is to rehearse and deliver a business workshop and score 10 out of 10 on every participant-feedback form, you may not succeed even if your workshop is outstanding. Some people may give you only a 9. You have absolutely no control over subjective things like people's opinions—but you do have control over taking the required actions for the goals you determine.

Train yourself to be accountable for your goals. Be honest with yourself about the consequences of pursuing or not pursuing them. Give them your very best efforts. And remember: You can't guarantee results, but you can measure the actions you take that are necessary for the results you want. Focus on the actions!

Bonus Step

I thought it would be fun to throw this in last.

Think of a reward you can give to yourself once you've achieved the steps necessary for your goal. If possible, try and make it something special to which you would not normally treat yourself. This step is not vital to your goal-setting system, but it's a nice perk and motivator to keep you on-track.

Don't "reinvent the wheel"

Secret 48

You'd think this bit of common-sense advice would not have to be repeated. It must, however—considering the number of times I've seen people develop a business project, process, or even a document from scratch when it hasn't been necessary.

There's a simple way to avoid this trap of "reinventing the wheel" (and often finding that the wheel doesn't work!). Simply model each new undertaking after a proven success. As the saying goes, "If you have time to do it over, you have the time to do it right the first time."

It just makes sense to take a step back and search for an existing template, or to speak with an expert, before charging into unknown territory. After a few embarrassing fumbles in this area, I resolved never to invent mediocrity again. My business has worked more efficiently ever since.

Secret 49

Negotiate effectively

A comprehensive guide to the art of negotiation is beyond the scope of this book. However, here is an outline of central concepts that should get you well on your way to being an effective negotiator.

If you're interested in taking your negotiation skills further, many good books, seminars, and workshops are available.

I. Determine three positions in advance

Before you enter into a negotiation where you are the one setting the price, take the time to calculate three positions:

1. **The lowest amount you will accept without negative consequences to your business.**

   Determining this number ahead of time is crucial, as it needs to be a sound business decision. Any less than this and you know in advance that you're 100% prepared to walk away from the deal.

2. **The price you would expect to get—the perfect middle ground.**

3. **The highest price you feel you can legitimately charge.**

   Observe the key word "legitimately"! You may be tempted to exploit an opportunity to charge too much, but it can come back to haunt you and potentially damage your credibility or reputation. It's not worth it.

II. Always lead with your highest price

Reasons for doing so include:

- The perceived value of your product or service goes up in the other person's mind. People typically equate a higher price with higher value or quality.

- If the other person starts negotiating the price, you have room to come down. Resist the temptation to start with your lowest price, as many unseasoned, unconfident businesspeople do. You'll have nowhere else to go!

- You may well get the price you ask for! As we've heard many times: If you don't ask for something, you'll never get it.

III. Don't give in too easily

If the person with whom you're negotiating tries to make you agree to major concessions, such as free service or an extended warranty, counter with something minor.

Don't make it too easy on them, or they won't feel like they won!

That's the psychological reality behind negotiating: If it comes too easy, we always feel we could have done better. We value those things we work hardest for. Always remember this key point.

Instead of immediately agreeing, you should be sure that *concessions are given on a basis of equal exchange.* Anything you give should be conditional on getting something in return, or you're not negotiating—and you're back to the point made above ("Don't make it too easy on them, or they won't feel like they've won").

The most effective way to do this is through effective use of the key words "if" and "then." For example:

"Well, if you were to give up _____ , then I could give you additional _____ ."

IV. When they counter your offer, ask them why

Rather than accepting their offer or immediately offering a counterproposal, try something unexpected—simply ask them why. For example:

"Okay, well let's talk about that. Why do you need that price?"

Last, but not least: Be patient and persistent. It will pay off.

Beta-test, beta-test, beta-test

I'm not trying to be redundant, but it's way too important *not* to repeat.

Secret 50

You can minimize the risk and cost of an unsuccessful endeavor by first testing it at the smallest scale possible. It's important to do a thorough beta test before deciding that a major new process is a go. That means you must take the time to go through all of its stages before you proceed.

In 1985, the Coca-Cola Company decided to replace their famous flagship product with a new formula they called New Coke. Unfortunately, their customers hated it. The company was forced to recall New Coke and return to original Coke, costing them millions in advertising, production expenses, and lost business. This could have been avoided with proper beta testing.

Coke's hard lesson shows why it's so important to experiment with new ideas before putting them into action. Consider making it your company policy *not* to dive into any new approach or venture without first conducting a beta test.

Hire specialists for crucial tasks

Secret 51

In crucial business areas, the cost of not purchasing the counsel and services of experts far outweighs the cost of doing so. Just ask some people who learned this the hard way—like me—and you'll see the light in a hurry.

As Secret 44 states, when making key business decisions, ask yourself:

1. What is the cost of doing it?

2. What is the cost of **not** doing it?

When selecting your experts, don't look at price alone. It may be tempting to engage a junior associate at a large firm, but they may not have the skills or experience to represent you and your business. Take your time, and be sure you're completely confident you have the right person.

Thank-you notes:
If you use them, here's the rule

Secret 52

Should you send thank-you notes to your customers? Opinions are divided. Some companies do it routinely; most don't send them at all.

To help you decide if thank-you notes should be part of your business culture, ask yourself if you've ever received a thank-you note from someone in appreciation for your business. If so—and if it was sent promptly— how did it make you feel? It likely wasn't the sole reason for your decision to buy again, or to be a lifelong customer; but did it affect your perception of the sender to some degree? Did it make you think the sender had a certain grace and class, a caring attitude? If so, was that important to you? It's your choice.

If you decide that thank-you notes fit your style, be sure to observe this rule: *Send them immediately, or not at all.* Few people appreciate a delayed thank-you. It can do more harm than good by making you seem disorganized—or worse, making it seem that you didn't consider the recipient a priority.

Use role models to stay motivated

Being a business-owner can have its moments. I recall some moments in the first year and a half of Marketshare and Approved Publications where things were at an all-time stress level.

Delayed accounts-receivable were the norm, it seemed, and my business partner and I were continually borrowing money. The 80- to 90-hour weeks, and the stress of meeting payroll, made me feel like I had it pretty rough.

What got me through it? When things got that way, I made a point of thinking about key people in my life whose struggles and challenges made mine seem insignificant. This perspective helped immensely. It allowed me to be grateful for my health and the amazing opportunity I had with the business. It fueled me to resume my work with renewed spirit and attitude. And we all know, "Our attitude determines our altitude."

My most inspiring model is my grandmother, Mrs. Ruth Hannaford. As I write these words in April, 2004, she is 96 years old and sharp as a whip. After my grandfather passed away, Ruth lived on her own until she was 95. Today she has to have a blood transfusion every 3 weeks, and faces other physical challenges as well. Yet she is always chipper and positive, and refuses to let her circumstances get her spirits down.

Bottom line? If she can maintain a positive attitude in her situation, I have absolutely nothing to complain about. I heartily recommend that you find your own source of inspiration so you can keep your spirits up when the road gets particularly rough.

Some Final Thoughts

Thank you for reading this book. Writing it has been a great experience for me—a challenge and a pleasure.

Like you, I'm a businessperson. I'm motivated by the goal of writing successful books. But there's always more to it than the money. If you use these "secrets" to achieve your business goals, I'll have the personal satisfaction of knowing that I made a difference in the quality of your life, and in the lives of those you care about.

Books can be treasure chests of information and advice, yet most people don't take advantage of them. Now that you've finished this book, you can be way ahead of the crowd—you have the tools you need for success.

Each of us has only one life to live. There are no replays. You can't stop the clock, go back, and do it over. At the end of their lives, most people regret the things they did *not* do more than the things they did.

So play with the goal of winning—because the only other option is a life of mediocrity. You're someone with the imagination and initiative to start your own business. I'm willing to bet that your vision for business success doesn't have the word "average" stamped on it.

I'll leave you with an observation that has always made me chuckle.

> **There are three kinds of people in the world:**
> **Those who make it happen,**
> **Those who watch it happen,**
> **And those who say, "Hey, what happened?"**

Good luck landing that Fortune 1000 client!

Sincerely,

MIKE

P.S.: In future editions of the Approved Series books, we will be including **real-life success stories** from Approved Series readers. If you feel that this book helped you get the results you were seeking, I would be delighted to hear from you. Please write to me here: **mike@approvedseries.com**

Resources for Small Business

U.S. Small Business Administration
www.sba.gov

Service Corps of Retired Executives (SCORE)
www.score.org

Business Gateway to Federal Resources
www.business.gov

Bizstats.Com (free business and educational resources)
www.bizstats.com

Free Trademark Search
www.uspto.gov

U.S. Chamber of Commerce Center for Small Business
www.uschamber.org

Trade Show Info
www.tsnn.com

Canadian Chamber of Commerce
www.chamber.ca

Canadian Business Service Centers
www.cbsc.org

Industry Canada
www.strategis.ic.gc.ca

Buyer Contributors

Greg Adkins Purchasing Manager
38

Lori Aljets Purchasing and Quality Assurance Manager,
Norpac Foods Inc.
57

Trent N. Baker, Purchasing Manager, Wilson Foods,
C.P.M. Division Of Reser's Fine Foods, Inc.
57, 95

Scott Bartel Sourcing Strategist
57

Beckie Beard, Director, Purchasing & Materials Management,
C.P.M, A.P.P., CACM Lansing Community College
107

Leslie Champion Senior Procurement Specialist
Industrial Design & Construction, Inc.
62

Andrew Jules Degiulio Purchasing Manager
77, 103

Krysia Diaz, Benefits Supervisor
CEBS 82

Wendy Imamura,
C.P.M., CPPB, CMIR
Material Processing Center Manager,
Verizon Hawaii Inc.
42

Peggy Jones
Operations/H.R. Director,
Magic Software Enterprises, Inc.
79

Mike Kanze,
MBA, C.P.M., A.P.P.
President, Cornerstone Services Incorporated
49, 60, 66

Natalie Levy
V.P. Divisional Merchandise Manager,
Lord And Taylor
60, 66

Christopher Locke
Global Lead Buyer, DaimlerChrysler Corporation
3, 29, 63

Tina M. Lowenthal
Associate Director, Purchasing Services,
California Institute of Technology
33

Richard Lusk
Director of Purchasing, Lennar Homes, Inc.
71

Paula L. Martin
Corporate IT Buyer
39, 42

Steve Mataya
Materials Manager,
Allied Gear & Machine Co. Inc.
60

Index

About the Author

Michael Schell spent 20 years in business-to-business sales, primarily in highly-competitive, commission-based industries, where he won numerous achievement awards. Michael is President and CEO of the Approved Group of Companies in Vancouver, British Columbia, including:

Approved Publications, Inc. (www.approvedpublicationsinc.com)

Approved Learning, Inc. (www.approvedlearninginc.com)

Marketshare Research Institute (www.marketshareresearch.com)

When Michael isn't writing books, being a keynote speaker, or working with his talented staff, he enjoys cycling, traveling, playing guitar with his rock band, and jumping out of perfectly good airplanes.

About the Research Director

Mitch Merker, Vice President and COO of the Approved Group of Companies, is an accomplished business professional with over 18 years of front-line sales and customer-service experience.

Mitch directs the Marketshare Research Institute, which provides Approved™ Series readers with the most current, practical business information available. Mitch also organizes Marketshare's custom research projects, and often appears as a guest speaker.

About the Approved™ Series

During his corporate sales career, author Michael Schell attended many sales seminars and workshops. He read hundreds of books on sales, business development, public speaking, and human relations. He often wondered:

- Why did authors and speakers take so much time to explain simple concepts, and to describe specific, practical ways to use them?
- How did the methods they recommended work in the real world?
- Where was the validation from the people who mattered most: the decision-makers?

Mike realized that the book he was looking for had not been written—a book from the perspective of the people who were *sold to*. These people had met and interacted with countless sales reps; they knew exactly what worked and what didn't. Who could explain selling better than professional buyers?

The result was *Buyer-Approved Selling*, a book filled with practical, no-nonsense approaches recommended by buyers from many companies across the U.S. This groundbreaking book has been embraced by the corporate community. Some businesses have ordered custom editions of it for their sales departments.

Mike has been invited to lead special **Buyer-Approved training seminars** and is in demand as a keynote speaker. Backed by the Approved Series's extensive research and his own first-hand knowledge of sales, Mike presents the Buyer-Approved sales concepts in a concrete, ready-to-use form that sales professionals can immediately apply to their work.

How the Approved™ Series works for you

The Approved Series focuses on the opinions of the decision-makers who are most important to you and your work:

You	Decision-makers	Approved Series Title
Sales representative	Professional buyers	*Buyer-Approved Selling*
Small-business owner	Corporate customers	*The Customer-Approved Small Business*
Job seeker	Employers	*Human Resource-Approved Job Interviews & Resumes*

Each Approved Series book gives you a complete step-by-step plan for achieving the results you seek, based on advice from the kinds of people you want to influence. In addition to the recommended methods, you'll read decision-makers' actual comments as they explain why some methods work and some fail. (The answers may surprise you!)

It's one thing to read a book, and another to apply it. You can use the Approved Series secrets with confidence, knowing they come from "the right side of the desk." It makes all the difference!

THE  SERIES

BUYER-APPROVED SELLING

The groundbreaking guide for sales professionals, based on interviews with hundreds of business buyers across the U.S. Includes clear step-by-step methods, buyers' actual comments, and worksheets for developing your own sales plans. Stop guessing—start selling the Approved™ way!

$19.95 US/$24.95 Canada

THE SALES STAR

The companion guide to *Buyer-Approved Selling*—in story form! Follow the success of Jack and Morena, two new sales reps, as they use Buyer-Approved methods to put their careers into high gear.

$14.95 US/$19.95 Canada

THE CUSTOMER-APPROVED SMALL BUSINESS

This easy-to-read, step-by-step guide shows you how to master the two requirements of a successful business:
(1) Creating a solid foundation for outstanding service
(2) Finding and keeping customers

$19.95 US/$24.95 Canada

HUMAN RESOURCE-APPROVED JOB INTERVIEWS & RESUMES

Do you wonder what employers *really* think of your cover letters and resumes? Do you want to make your best impression at interviews? This easy-to-read, easy-to-use book gives you the practical advice you need—direct from H.R. professionals themselves.

$19.95 US/$24.95 Canada

More titles coming soon!

Contact us about:

- Using the Approved Series for corporate promotions
- Customized books, booklets, and book excerpts
- Bulk orders • Keynote speakers
- Approved Learning workshops

Call toll free: **877-870-0009**

Visit us online at **www.approvedseries.com**